I0018304

Google Drive Made Simple
A Beginner's Handbook

Kiet Huynh

Table of Contents

Introduction

1.1 What is Google Drive?

 Google Drive is a cloud-based storage service developed by Google that allows users to store files, access them from multiple devices, and share them with others easily. Introduced in 2012, Google Drive has grown to become a cornerstone of productivity for millions of people worldwide, offering an intuitive platform to organize and manage digital content.

The Basics of Google Drive

At its core, Google Drive provides a digital "drive" where users can save files, including documents, photos, videos, and even complex data sets. Unlike traditional hard drives that store data on a physical computer, Google Drive operates in the cloud, meaning your files are stored on Google's secure servers. This feature enables users to access their data from anywhere with an internet connection, whether they're using a smartphone, tablet, or computer.

Google Drive also integrates seamlessly with other Google Workspace tools, such as Google Docs, Sheets, Slides, and Gmail, making it a versatile and powerful platform for both personal and professional use.

Key Features of Google Drive

1. Cloud Storage

Google Drive offers a reliable space for storing your files. Each user begins with 15 GB of free storage, which is shared across Google Drive, Gmail, and Google Photos. If more space is needed, Google provides paid plans through Google One, with options ranging from 100 GB to several terabytes.

2. File Accessibility

One of Google Drive's standout features is its accessibility. You can start working on a document on your home computer, make edits on your mobile phone during your commute, and present it using your office laptop—all without needing to transfer files manually.

3. Seamless Integration with Google Workspace

Google Drive is not just a storage platform; it's also the foundation for a suite of productivity tools. These include:

- **Google Docs:** A word processor for creating and editing text documents.

- **Google Sheets:** A spreadsheet tool for organizing data and performing calculations.

- **Google Slides:** A presentation software for designing slideshows. These tools work directly within Google Drive, allowing users to create, edit, and save files without needing additional software.

4. File Sharing and Collaboration

Google Drive makes collaboration effortless. Users can share files or folders with specific individuals, teams, or the public. With features like real-time editing and commenting, multiple users can work on the same document simultaneously, increasing efficiency and reducing the need for endless email chains.

5. Version Control

A lesser-known yet incredibly useful feature of Google Drive is version history. It allows users to view and restore previous versions of a file. This is particularly useful for collaborative projects where changes might need to be tracked or undone.

How Google Drive Differs from Traditional Storage Solutions

1. Portability

Unlike external hard drives or USB sticks, Google Drive eliminates the need for physical storage devices. As long as you have an internet connection, your files are just a few clicks away.

2. Automatic Backups

Google Drive protects your data by automatically saving changes in real-time. If your device crashes or gets lost, your files remain safe in the cloud.

3. Scalability

With physical storage, upgrading often requires purchasing new hardware. Google Drive's storage can be expanded instantly by upgrading your Google One plan, offering greater flexibility.

Use Cases of Google Drive

1. Personal Use

For individuals, Google Drive is a hub for organizing personal documents, photos, and videos. It's also a great platform for keeping backups of important files, such as travel itineraries or financial records.

2. Education

In educational settings, Google Drive empowers students and teachers to collaborate on assignments and projects. Its integration with tools like Google Classroom makes it a key component of modern digital learning.

3. Professional Settings

Businesses use Google Drive to streamline team collaboration and document management. Features like shared drives, granular permission settings, and integrations with productivity apps make it ideal for organizations of all sizes.

4. Creative Projects

Google Drive serves as a versatile platform for creatives, allowing them to store large media files, share drafts with clients, and access their work from multiple devices.

The Evolution of Google Drive

Google Drive has continually evolved since its inception, adding new features and improving its user experience. Over the years, Google has introduced artificial intelligence (AI) enhancements to help users organize files, such as the "Priority" feature, which surfaces the documents you're most likely to need.

Additionally, Google Drive has expanded its collaboration tools, introduced offline functionality, and improved security measures, cementing its status as a leader in the cloud storage space.

Why Google Drive is Essential in Today's World

In a world where remote work, online education, and digital collaboration are the norms, tools like Google Drive are no longer optional—they're essential. Google Drive provides a central platform for storing, sharing, and working on files, making it invaluable for individuals and teams alike.

Key reasons why Google Drive stands out include:

- **Convenience:** Access your files from anywhere.

- **Collaboration:** Work with others in real time.

- **Security:** Enjoy peace of mind knowing your files are stored safely.

Conclusion

Google Drive is more than just a cloud storage solution; it's a dynamic tool that enhances productivity, collaboration, and organization. Whether you're a student organizing your coursework, a professional managing team projects, or a creative working on your next masterpiece, Google Drive has something to offer.

In the following sections of this handbook, we'll explore how to maximize your use of Google Drive, from setting up your account to leveraging advanced features. By the end of this guide, you'll be equipped with all the knowledge you need to use Google Drive effectively.

1.2 Why Use Google Drive?

In today's digital world, managing files and collaborating on projects has become more complex than ever before. With the rise of cloud computing, traditional storage methods have become outdated, inefficient, and prone to data loss. That's where Google Drive comes in. But why, you may ask, should you use Google Drive specifically? This section will explain the compelling reasons why Google Drive has become the go-to solution for millions of individuals and businesses alike.

Cloud-Based Convenience

One of the most significant advantages of Google Drive is that it is a cloud-based storage system. This means you can access your files from any device, at any time, as long as you have an internet connection. Gone are the days of having to carry around a USB drive or worry about running out of storage space on your computer. Whether you're on a laptop, tablet, or smartphone, Google Drive ensures that your files are always available at your fingertips.

Cloud storage offers tremendous flexibility. For example, if you're working on a project and need to reference a file while you're away from your office, all you need is an internet connection and your Google account. No more scrambling to find the right folder or worrying about whether your USB drive is still plugged in. You can even access your files while on vacation, in a meeting, or during a commute, which is ideal for individuals who need to stay productive on the go.

Seamless Collaboration

One of the most powerful features of Google Drive is its ability to facilitate real-time collaboration. Whether you're working on a group project, a presentation, or a shared document, Google Drive allows you and your collaborators to work on the same file simultaneously. Multiple users can open the same document, spreadsheet, or presentation, and make changes that are immediately reflected on everyone's screen. This eliminates the need for sending files back and forth via email, drastically improving efficiency.

For example, imagine you're working with a team on a proposal. With Google Drive, you can all edit the document together, providing feedback, making revisions, and adding your own sections without worrying about version control. You'll always have the most up-to-date version of the document, with no need to track changes or send multiple drafts. This collaborative experience extends to Google Sheets and Google Slides as well, making it easy to work together on data analysis or presentations in real time.

Moreover, Google Drive allows users to leave comments on specific sections of a document, making it easier to communicate within the file itself. You can tag others in comments, ask for input, or simply provide clarification. This level of collaboration is incredibly helpful for teams, students, and anyone working with others on a shared project.

Enhanced Accessibility and Mobility

Another standout feature of Google Drive is its accessibility. It's not just for desktops or laptops anymore. Google Drive offers apps for both Android and iOS, ensuring that your files are always accessible, no matter where you are. Whether you need to review a document while sitting on the bus, upload photos from your phone, or share a presentation before a meeting starts, Google Drive is designed to be with you every step of the way.

The mobile app even allows you to view, edit, and share documents, which means you can remain productive even when you're away from your computer. For users who are constantly on the move or prefer to use mobile devices for most tasks, this level of accessibility is invaluable.

Moreover, Google Drive's offline mode allows users to access and edit their files without an internet connection. This feature is perfect for times when you may be traveling or in an area with limited connectivity. Once you reconnect to the internet, any changes made offline are automatically synced, keeping everything up to date across your devices.

Ample Free Storage

Google Drive offers users 15 GB of free storage, which is more than sufficient for storing a significant number of documents, photos, and small video files. For many users, this free storage is more than enough, and they can use Google Drive without ever having to worry about hitting a storage cap. For example, 15 GB is enough to store thousands of documents, hundreds of spreadsheets, and dozens of presentations. Google Drive's efficient storage management ensures that you can easily monitor your usage and manage files to optimize available space.

If you ever run out of space, Google offers affordable options for additional storage through its Google One subscription plans. These plans allow you to expand your storage and even share it across multiple Google services, including Gmail and Google Photos.

This level of flexibility makes Google Drive a cost-effective solution for personal and professional storage needs.

Integration with Google's Ecosystem

Another compelling reason to use Google Drive is its seamless integration with the broader Google ecosystem. Google Drive works smoothly with Google's other widely-used tools, such as Gmail, Google Docs, Google Sheets, Google Slides, and Google Meet. When you attach a file from Google Drive to an email in Gmail, for instance, you don't have to worry about size limits or attachment issues. You can simply share a link to the file, and the recipient can access it immediately.

For collaborative work, integration with Google Docs, Sheets, and Slides means you can easily create and edit documents within Drive, with everything auto-saved as you go. This eliminates the fear of losing work due to unexpected shutdowns or crashes. Similarly, the integration of Google Meet within Google Drive allows you to schedule and attend video meetings, directly collaborating with others on the same documents and spreadsheets in real-time.

Google Drive's integration also extends to third-party applications through Google Workspace Marketplace, where you can find apps that suit your specific needs. These apps can be added directly to Google Drive, enhancing your productivity and expanding its capabilities. Whether you need a tool for project management, photo editing, or note-taking, the variety of compatible apps means that Google Drive can easily be customized to suit your workflow.

Robust File Sharing and Security Features

File sharing is another area where Google Drive shines. Not only does it make sharing simple and intuitive, but it also gives users fine control over permissions. When you share a file or folder on Google Drive, you can choose whether recipients can view, comment, or edit the file. This ensures that sensitive information is protected while allowing for the necessary collaboration.

Google Drive also offers advanced security features to protect your files. All files stored on Google Drive are encrypted, and Google takes additional steps to ensure your data remains secure. Google's two-factor authentication adds another layer of protection for your account, giving you peace of mind knowing that your files are safeguarded from unauthorized access.

Moreover, Google Drive makes it easy to track changes to shared files. The version history feature allows you to see all changes made to a document, and you can revert to previous versions if needed. This feature is particularly valuable for teams or individuals who work with large documents or frequently collaborate on a single file.

A Reliable Backup Solution

Google Drive offers an easy and reliable backup solution. If you're concerned about losing important files, Google Drive can serve as your digital safety net. Once you upload your files to Google Drive, they're backed up in the cloud, so even if your computer crashes or your device is lost, your data remains safe. Files stored on Google Drive can be accessed from anywhere, meaning your documents are never truly lost, as long as you have access to your Google account.

In addition to providing a reliable backup, Google Drive makes file recovery straightforward. Whether you accidentally deleted a file or made unwanted changes, Google Drive's robust file recovery system lets you restore lost or overwritten files with ease.

Cost-Effectiveness

For individuals, Google Drive is free to use, offering an ample 15 GB of storage at no cost. This makes it an extremely cost-effective solution for those who need to store files, collaborate with others, or access documents on the go. For businesses and organizations, Google Drive's premium offerings, such as Google Workspace, provide a range of features tailored for enterprises, including advanced administrative controls, more storage, and collaboration tools.

The value for money that Google Drive offers is hard to beat. Whether you are an individual or part of a larger organization, the cost-to-benefit ratio makes Google Drive an appealing choice for anyone looking for efficient, secure, and user-friendly cloud storage.

1.3 Who is This Book For?

In today's fast-paced digital world, cloud storage and collaboration tools have become an essential part of both our personal and professional lives. Google Drive, one of the most popular and powerful cloud platforms available, is designed to make storing, sharing, and collaborating on files easier than ever. But with its variety of features and options, it can be overwhelming for those who are new to it.

This book, *Google Drive Made Simple: A Beginner's Handbook*, is specifically written for individuals who are either completely new to Google Drive or those who have heard of its benefits but need guidance on how to navigate it efficiently. If you find yourself in any of the following categories, this book is made for you:

Beginners to Cloud Storage

Perhaps you've never used cloud storage before, or you've only used it sparingly and never fully explored its features. You might be someone who's used to saving files on your computer or physical devices and is unsure about making the switch to cloud-based tools. If you're overwhelmed by the idea of storing your files online, syncing data, or understanding how cloud storage works, you'll find that this book introduces Google Drive in a simple, easy-to-understand manner.

The beauty of Google Drive is that it's not just for tech-savvy individuals. It's for everyone, from people who simply want to store documents to those who need advanced features like collaboration and file sharing. We'll start from the basics, walking you through everything you need to know to set up, organize, and manage your files in the cloud.

Busy Professionals

In the workplace, time is always in short supply. Professionals often juggle multiple tasks, projects, and deadlines. For many, the challenge is not just managing information but organizing and accessing it in an efficient manner. Google Drive can help alleviate this burden by allowing you to store files securely online, share them with others in real-time, and work collaboratively on documents and spreadsheets.

If you're a professional who's often on the go or someone who works with teams spread across different locations, this book will show you how Google Drive can be a game-changer. With Google Drive's ability to sync files across devices, you'll never have to worry about not having access to the latest versions of your work. Plus, you'll learn to leverage Google Drive's collaboration tools, so you can work on projects simultaneously with colleagues, clients, or partners no matter where they are located.

This book provides you with step-by-step guidance on how to get started with Google Drive for your professional needs, focusing on productivity features that can streamline your work processes.

Students and Educators

Students at every level – from high school to university – are increasingly using digital tools to manage their assignments, research papers, and collaborative projects. Educators also find Google Drive useful for creating and sharing resources with students, providing feedback on assignments, and maintaining class records. Google Drive is not just a tool for file storage, it's also a dynamic platform that fosters communication, collaboration, and creative work among students and teachers alike.

If you're a student who wants to store your work securely online, collaborate with classmates, or keep track of research materials, this book will show you how to make the most of Google Drive's tools. You'll learn how to create and organize your documents, presentations, and spreadsheets in a way that maximizes your productivity. Additionally, as an educator, you'll find helpful tips on how to integrate Google Drive into your teaching methods, such as sharing assignments, providing real-time feedback, and collaborating with other educators on projects.

Individuals Looking to Organize Personal Files

In our personal lives, we often accumulate an overwhelming amount of digital files. Photos, videos, documents, and emails can quickly clutter our computers and mobile devices. Google Drive offers an easy way to organize these files into categories, ensuring that you can access important documents at a moment's notice. Whether you need to keep track of personal finances, organize family photos, or store important records for safekeeping, Google Drive provides a flexible space for all types of personal file storage.

This book will guide you through creating a well-organized digital filing system on Google Drive, so you can manage your personal documents more effectively. You'll also discover how to take advantage of Google Drive's search capabilities, allowing you to locate any file instantly, even if you have hundreds or thousands of items stored.

Freelancers and Small Business Owners

Freelancers and small business owners face unique challenges when it comes to managing files and collaborating with clients. Often, there's no formal infrastructure like a large company would have, so everything from contracts and invoices to client deliverables needs to be managed independently. Google Drive is an excellent solution for freelancers and small business owners looking for an affordable, easy-to-use platform that allows them to store, share, and collaborate on files in a professional and organized way.

If you're a freelancer, this book will teach you how to set up an efficient filing system for your business, manage contracts, invoices, and client communications, and collaborate on documents with clients. You'll also learn how to set up Google Drive to sync across devices, ensuring that you have access to your business files no matter where you are working from.

For small business owners, we'll walk you through using Google Drive for managing internal documents, sharing marketing materials with your team, and collaborating on client projects. Google Drive's accessibility, low cost, and real-time collaboration features make it the perfect solution for entrepreneurs and business owners looking to streamline their operations.

Individuals Who Want to Collaborate Effectively

Collaboration is one of the key strengths of Google Drive. Whether you're working on a team project at work, participating in a group assignment at school, or planning an event with family and friends, Google Drive makes it easy to collaborate with others. With real-time editing, commenting, and sharing features, everyone involved in a project can stay on the same page and contribute seamlessly.

If you're someone who frequently works with others and needs a reliable tool to collaborate on documents, spreadsheets, or presentations, this book is for you. We'll show you how to set up shared folders, manage access permissions, and track changes to ensure smooth collaboration every time. Whether you're working with colleagues, clients, classmates, or friends, Google Drive's powerful collaboration tools will enhance your productivity and help you achieve better results.

People Seeking to Enhance Their Digital Literacy

Even if you're not sure if you fall into one of the specific categories mentioned above, this book is for anyone who wants to improve their digital literacy. Learning how to use Google Drive effectively is a great way to familiarize yourself with cloud storage, file management, and digital collaboration tools that are becoming more common in today's interconnected world.

If you've always been curious about how cloud storage works but felt intimidated by it, or if you want to be more comfortable with digital tools in general, this book will help you build confidence. By the end of this guide, you'll have a solid understanding of how Google Drive works, how to use it to organize your digital life, and how to take full advantage of its powerful features.

Conclusion

Ultimately, *Google Drive Made Simple: A Beginner's Handbook* is for anyone who wants to learn how to use Google Drive in a practical and efficient way. Whether you're a student, a professional, a freelancer, or just someone looking to better organize your personal files, this book will provide you with the knowledge and skills you need to harness the power of Google Drive. We aim to simplify the learning process and offer clear, actionable guidance that will help you make the most of this versatile cloud storage solution.

1.4 How to Use This Handbook

Whether you're completely new to cloud storage or have dabbled in Google Drive before, this book is designed to guide you through every step of using Google Drive effectively. With a focus on simplicity and clarity, you will find comprehensive instructions, helpful tips, and practical examples that will enable you to harness the full power of Google Drive.

In this section, we will walk through how to make the most of this handbook and ensure that you get the information you need at every stage of your learning journey.

Navigating the Structure of the Book

To begin, let's first examine the structure of this handbook. It is divided into chapters, each focusing on a specific aspect of Google Drive. The book starts with the basics, such as setting up your Google account and exploring the interface. As we progress, we delve into more advanced topics, like organizing your files, collaborating with others, and leveraging Google Drive's various features for maximum productivity.

Each chapter is designed to be self-contained, meaning that you can easily refer to any section without needing to read the entire book from start to finish. If you are just starting with Google Drive, we recommend reading from Chapter 1 onward, gradually building up your knowledge and confidence. If you're already familiar with the basics but want to learn about specific features, you can jump directly to the relevant chapter.

Step-by-Step Instructions and Clear Examples

This handbook uses a step-by-step approach to guide you through each feature of Google Drive. Wherever possible, we've included clear, easy-to-follow examples, screenshots, and instructions that will help you understand how each tool or function works.

For instance, when explaining how to upload a file, we'll walk you through the process with instructions like:

1. Click on the "New" button on the left side of your Google Drive.

2. Select "File upload" from the dropdown menu.

3. Choose the file from your computer that you wish to upload.

Each of these steps is explained in simple language to ensure that even beginners can follow along with ease.

Learning by Doing

One of the most effective ways to learn is through hands-on experience. As you go through the book, we encourage you to open Google Drive and try out the instructions as you read. This will help reinforce the concepts and make them easier to remember.

In fact, each chapter includes "Try It Yourself" sections, where you can apply what you've learned by performing specific tasks or exercises. These activities will give you the chance to get comfortable with Google Drive and build your skills progressively.

For example, after learning how to create a folder, the "Try It Yourself" section might ask you to create a folder, upload a document into it, and share the folder with a colleague. This allows you to practice what you've just read and to see how the features come together in real-world scenarios.

Tips for Faster Learning

While this handbook is designed to be straightforward, some features of Google Drive may take a little extra time to master. Don't worry! Learning any new software can feel overwhelming at first, but with a few strategies in place, you can make the process much smoother:

1. **Break It Down:** Google Drive is a powerful tool with many features. It's helpful to take things one step at a time. If a chapter feels too dense, try breaking it down into smaller sections and revisiting it later.

2. **Revisit Sections:** If you're unsure about a concept, feel free to return to previous chapters and review key points. You may find that revisiting a topic after learning something new will help solidify your understanding.

3. **Use the Search Function:** Google Drive has a robust search function, and you should use it as a valuable resource when learning. Similarly, the index and table of contents in this book are designed to make it easy for you to find exactly what you're looking for.

4. **Ask for Help:** If you're stuck, don't hesitate to ask for help. There are many online forums and communities where you can find support. Google's official help site and Google Drive's own support tools are also excellent resources when you need quick answers to your questions.

5. **Take Your Time:** Finally, remember that this is a learning journey. Don't rush through the book. Take your time to experiment with the features and absorb the

information at your own pace. Everyone learns differently, and it's okay to take breaks or revisit sections as needed.

The Importance of Experimentation

As you read through this book, you'll encounter a variety of Google Drive's features, from file sharing to using Google Docs and Google Sheets directly in Drive. While the instructions will guide you step-by-step, the key to truly mastering Google Drive lies in experimentation.

For example, once you've learned how to create a Google Doc, try adding some formatting to it or inserting images. Explore the various options in the toolbar to familiarize yourself with all the tools available. Experiment with uploading different types of files, like PDFs, images, and videos, to see how Google Drive handles them.

Experimenting in this way will help you become more comfortable with Google Drive's features and capabilities, making you more efficient in your work. Don't be afraid to click around and try things out — you'll be amazed at how much you can learn just by experimenting on your own.

How to Utilize the "Try It Yourself" Sections

Each chapter features a section dedicated to practical exercises called "Try It Yourself." These exercises are designed to encourage you to apply what you've learned in real-time. They typically follow each new topic and are intended to reinforce your skills.

Here's how to make the most out of these sections:

1. **Complete the exercises after reading through the chapter:** Don't skip them! They are a crucial part of the learning process.

2. **Start small:** If the exercise asks you to perform several actions, break it down into manageable steps. Focus on one task at a time.

3. **Check your progress:** After completing an exercise, go back and verify whether you achieved the desired result. Did you successfully upload a file? Can you share it with a colleague? If not, review the instructions again and give it another try.

By actively engaging with the exercises, you'll gain practical experience that will make you feel more confident in using Google Drive.

Using This Book for Ongoing Reference

While this book is structured to take you from beginner to proficient Google Drive user, it can also serve as a valuable reference tool long after you've finished reading it. Once you've completed the chapters and exercises, you might find yourself needing to look up specific features or options in the future.

Each chapter is organized logically, with clear headings and subheadings that allow you to quickly find the information you need. Whether you're looking for a specific tip on organizing your files or trying to remember how to create a shared folder, you'll be able to easily navigate back to the relevant section in the book.

In addition to using the table of contents, the index at the end of the book will be an invaluable resource. If you need help with a particular Google Drive term, action, or feature, simply look it up in the index to find the exact page number where it's discussed.

Beyond the Book: Continuing Your Google Drive Journey

Learning how to use Google Drive is just the beginning. Once you're comfortable with the basics, we encourage you to continue exploring and discovering new ways to maximize its potential. Google Drive is constantly evolving, with new features and updates being added regularly. This means that your journey with Google Drive doesn't have to end once you finish this book.

To keep your skills fresh and up to date, we recommend visiting the Google Drive Help Center, checking out blog posts from Google, and joining Google's online communities. These resources will provide you with tips, tutorials, and discussions about the latest features.

Additionally, Google often updates Drive's interface and functionality, so don't be surprised if some things look different in the future. However, the fundamentals you learn in this book will remain valuable as you adapt to new versions of the platform.

Conclusion

By following the guidance in this handbook, you'll be well on your way to becoming a proficient Google Drive user. Remember, the key to success is consistent practice, hands-on experience, and the willingness to explore new features as they become available. Whether you use Google Drive for personal organization or professional collaboration, this powerful tool will make managing your files easier and more efficient than ever before.

We hope that this book will empower you to take full advantage of Google Drive and transform the way you work, collaborate, and store your files. Happy learning!

CHAPTER I
Getting Started with Google Drive

1.1 Setting Up Your Google Account

Setting up a Google Account is the first and most essential step to accessing Google Drive and other Google services. This chapter will guide you through the process, ensuring you're fully equipped to begin your journey with Google Drive.

Why You Need a Google Account

A Google Account is your gateway to a suite of powerful tools, including Google Drive, Gmail, Google Calendar, and more. With a single account, you gain access to an integrated ecosystem that simplifies your digital life. Moreover, your Google Account allows you to:

- Store and manage files in Google Drive.

- Collaborate in real-time with others.

- Access your files from any device, anywhere.

Step 1: Creating a Google Account

Follow these steps to create your Google Account:

1. **Visit the Sign-Up Page:**

    o Open a web browser and go to https://accounts.google.com/signup.

2. **Fill in Your Personal Details:**

    o Enter your first and last name.

- o Create a unique username. This will be your Gmail address (e.g., yourname@gmail.com). If your preferred username is taken, Google will suggest alternatives or allow you to choose a different one.

- o Set a secure password. A strong password should include a mix of uppercase and lowercase letters, numbers, and special characters.

3. **Provide Recovery Information:**

   - o Add your phone number and an alternate email address for account recovery. These details help secure your account and allow you to recover it if you forget your password.

4. **Agree to Google's Terms:**

   - o Review Google's terms of service and privacy policy. Click "I agree" to proceed.

5. **Verify Your Identity:**

   - o Google may ask you to verify your phone number. You'll receive a code via text or call that you need to enter on the website.

Once these steps are complete, you have successfully created your Google Account.

Step 2: Securing Your Account

Creating an account is just the beginning. Keeping it secure is equally important. Here are some tips to protect your Google Account:

1. **Enable Two-Factor Authentication (2FA):**

   o Two-factor authentication adds an extra layer of security. Every time you sign in, you'll need to enter a code sent to your phone.

   o To enable 2FA, go to your account settings, select "Security," and follow the prompts under "2-Step Verification."

2. **Choose a Strong Password:**

   o Avoid using common passwords like "123456" or "password." Instead, use a combination of random words, numbers, and symbols.

3. **Monitor Account Activity:**

   o Regularly check your account activity to spot unauthorized access. Google provides a dashboard that shows recent logins, devices, and locations.

Step 3: Customizing Your Google Account

After setting up your account, you can customize it to fit your preferences:

1. **Set Up Your Profile Picture:**

    o Adding a profile picture personalizes your account and makes it easier for collaborators to recognize you.

    o To upload a picture, click on your account icon in the top-right corner and select "Change."

2. **Manage Notifications:**

    o Adjust notification settings to stay informed without being overwhelmed.

    o Navigate to "Settings" in Google Drive or Gmail to control email and app notifications.

3. **Choose Your Default Language:**

    o Google supports multiple languages. Go to "Settings" > "Language" to select the one you're most comfortable with.

Step 4: Linking Your Account to Devices

Your Google Account can sync across devices, providing seamless access to your files:

1. **On Your Smartphone:**

    o Download the Google Drive app from the Google Play Store (Android) or the App Store (iOS).

    o Sign in using your new Google Account credentials.

2. **On Your Computer:**

    o For better file synchronization, install "Google Drive for Desktop." This app allows you to sync files directly from your computer to the cloud.

Common Issues During Account Setup

Sometimes, you might encounter problems while creating your account. Here's how to address them:

1. **Username Already Taken:**

- o   Try variations of your preferred username by adding numbers, middle initials, or alternate spellings.

2. **Verification Issues:**

    - o   Ensure your phone number is active and capable of receiving texts or calls. If you don't receive a code, request it again after checking your connection.

3. **Forgotten Password During Setup:**

    - o   If you forget your password during setup, click "Forgot Password" and follow the recovery process.

Conclusion

Setting up your Google Account is a straightforward but critical process that opens the door to a wide range of features, including Google Drive. By following the steps outlined in this section, you're well on your way to harnessing the power of Google's tools. In the next section, we'll explore how to access Google Drive and navigate its intuitive interface.

1.2 Accessing Google Drive

Accessing Google Drive is an essential first step in leveraging its powerful capabilities for organizing, storing, and sharing your files. Whether you are using a computer, smartphone, or tablet, Google Drive provides a seamless experience. This section will guide you through the process of accessing Google Drive across various devices and platforms, ensuring that you can start using it with ease.

Accessing Google Drive on a Desktop or Laptop

One of the most common ways to access Google Drive is through a web browser on your computer. Here's how you can do it:

1. **Open Your Browser**
   Google Drive is compatible with most popular web browsers, including Google Chrome, Mozilla Firefox, Microsoft Edge, and Safari. Open your preferred browser.

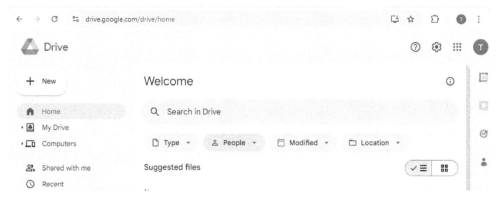

2. **Navigate to the Google Drive Website**
   Type https://drive.google.com in the address bar and press Enter. This will take you to the Google Drive homepage.

3. **Sign In to Your Google Account**
   If you're not already signed in, you'll be prompted to log in. Enter your Google account email and password, then click **Next**. If you have two-factor authentication enabled, complete the verification process.

4. **Explore the Drive Interface**

   Once logged in, you'll see the Google Drive interface, where you can start creating, uploading, and managing files.

Tips for Optimizing Your Web Experience

- **Bookmark the Drive Page**: Save the Drive homepage as a bookmark in your browser for quick access.

- **Enable Sync in Chrome**: If you use Google Chrome, logging into your Google account will automatically link Drive to the browser.

- **Incognito Mode**: To access Drive from a shared or public computer, use Incognito Mode to ensure your account remains secure.

Accessing Google Drive on Mobile Devices

Google Drive's mobile app provides flexibility for accessing your files anytime and anywhere. Follow these steps to get started:

1. **Download the Google Drive App**

   o **For Android Users**: Open the Google Play Store, search for "Google Drive," and tap **Install**.

   o **For iOS Users**: Open the App Store, search for "Google Drive," and tap **Get**.

2. **Log In to Your Google Account**

   Once installed, open the app and log in with your Google account credentials.

3. **Navigate the Mobile Interface**

   o **Home Tab**: Displays your most recent files and suggestions.

   o **Files Tab**: Shows a complete list of your stored items.

   o **Search Bar**: Quickly locate files using keywords.

4. **Syncing Files Across Devices**

Files you upload or edit on your mobile app will automatically sync with Google Drive on your desktop, ensuring seamless file management.

Features Exclusive to the Mobile App

- **Offline Access**: Mark files as "Available Offline" to view them without an internet connection.

- **Camera Integration**: Quickly upload photos or scan documents directly from your phone's camera.

Using Google Drive on Tablets

Tablets provide a balance between the mobility of smartphones and the functionality of desktops. Accessing Google Drive on tablets is similar to smartphones but with a few additional features:

1. **Install the Google Drive App**

   Download and install the app as you would on a smartphone.

2. **Enjoy Enhanced Productivity**

   Larger screens on tablets allow you to view and edit files more comfortably, making them ideal for tasks like reviewing presentations or working on spreadsheets.

3. **Multi-Window Functionality**

   Use multi-window or split-screen mode to work on a document in Google Drive while referencing a different app.

Accessing Google Drive Through the Google Workspace

If you are using Google Drive as part of Google Workspace (formerly G Suite), the process of accessing it integrates seamlessly with other tools like Gmail, Google Calendar, and Google Docs:

1. **Open Google Workspace Apps**

From the app launcher (the grid icon in the top-right corner of most Google services), select **Drive** to access your files.

2. **Switching Between Personal and Work Accounts**

If you have multiple Google accounts, use the profile icon in the top-right corner to switch between accounts. This is particularly useful for separating personal and professional documents.

Offline Access to Google Drive

Google Drive offers the ability to access your files without an internet connection. Here's how to set it up:

1. **Enable Offline Mode on Desktop**

   o   Open Google Drive in Chrome.

   o   Click the gear icon (Settings) in the top-right corner and select **Settings**.

   o   Under the **Offline** section, check the box labeled "Create, open, and edit your recent Google Docs, Sheets, and Slides files while offline."

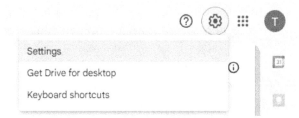

2. **Enable Offline Access on Mobile**

   o   Open the Google Drive app.

   o   Tap the three-dot menu next to a file or folder and select **Make Available Offline**.

3. **Limitations of Offline Mode**

   o   Offline access is primarily available for Google Docs, Sheets, and Slides. Non-Google file formats (e.g., PDFs) may need to be downloaded separately.

← Settings

General
Notifications
Manage apps

Appearance

◉ Light

○ Dark

○ Device default

Density

◉ Comfortable

○ Cozy

○ Compact

Open PDFs

○ New tab

◉ Preview

Uploads

☐ Convert uploads to Google Docs editor format

Offline

☐ Create, open and edit your recent Google Docs, Sheets, and Slides files on this device while offline

Not recommended on public or shared computers. Learn more

Best Practices for Offline Access

- Ensure your device has enough storage space to save offline files.

- Regularly reconnect to the internet to sync changes.

Troubleshooting Access Issues

Occasionally, you may encounter difficulties accessing Google Drive. Here are some common problems and solutions:

1. **Forgotten Password**

   o Use the "Forgot Password?" link on the sign-in page to reset your credentials.

2. **Browser Compatibility Issues**

   o Ensure your browser is updated to the latest version.

   o Clear your cache and cookies if you experience slow loading times.

3. **Mobile App Crashes**

   o Restart your device and update the app to the latest version.

   o Check for available storage space on your device.

4. **Network Connectivity Problems**

   o Verify that you have a stable internet connection.

   o Switch between Wi-Fi and mobile data if one network is unreliable.

By following the steps outlined above, you'll be equipped to access Google Drive effortlessly across all your devices. This flexibility ensures that your files are always at your fingertips, empowering you to work efficiently, whether at home, in the office, or on the go.

1.3 Navigating the Interface

1.3.1 The Home Screen

The **Home Screen** is the first thing you see when you open Google Drive. It serves as the central hub for all your files, folders, and tools. Understanding this interface is key to using Google Drive efficiently. In this section, we'll break down each element of the Home Screen, explain its purpose, and provide tips to help you navigate smoothly.

Overview of the Home Screen

When you first open Google Drive, the Home Screen is designed to present you with quick access to your most important or recently accessed files. Here's what you'll typically see:

1. **Search Bar**

   Located prominently at the top of the screen, the search bar allows you to find files, folders, or even specific content within documents. Google Drive's powerful search engine supports filters such as file type, owner, and modification date.

Tips for Effective Searches:

   o   Use keywords from the document name or content.

   o   Click the **filter icon** in the search bar to refine your search by file type, owner, or shared status.

   o   Use operators like "type:pdf" or "owner:me" to narrow results.

2. **Quick Access Section**
   Below the search bar, you'll find the **Quick Access** panel. This area shows files you've recently opened or edited, making it easy to resume your work without manually locating the file.

Customizing Quick Access:

   o   Enable or disable this feature in the settings menu if it doesn't suit your workflow.

   o   Pin frequently used files for consistent access.

3. **Main File Display Area**

   This section occupies the largest portion of the Home Screen. Depending on your settings or the view you select, this area will display your files in either a **list view** or **grid view**.

List View vs. Grid View:

   o   **List View:** Provides detailed information, including file name, owner, last modified date, and size.

   o   **Grid View:** Displays files as thumbnails, which is useful for visual recognition, especially for images and presentations.

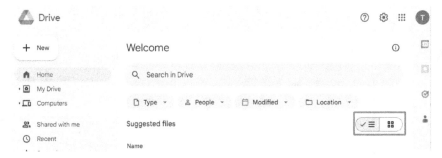

4. **Navigation Sidebar**
   While we'll dive deeper into the sidebar in **Section 1.3.2**, it's worth noting that the sidebar on the Home Screen provides shortcuts to essential sections like **My Drive**, **Shared with Me**, and **Trash**.

5. **Settings and Account Menu**

   In the top-right corner of the Home Screen, you'll find icons for:

o **Settings (gear icon):** Adjust preferences for notifications, offline access, and more.

o **Google Account:** Switch between accounts or manage account settings.

o **Help (question mark icon):** Access guides and troubleshooting support.

Detailed Features of the Home Screen

Search Bar Functionality

The search bar is not just a simple tool for locating files—it's a dynamic feature that integrates with Google's advanced algorithms. Beyond basic searches, the search bar supports natural language inputs like "Files shared by John last week."

Customizing Your Home Screen

To make your Home Screen more personalized:

- Adjust the display density (Compact, Comfortable, or Default).

- Organize your workspace by rearranging or hiding Quick Access files.

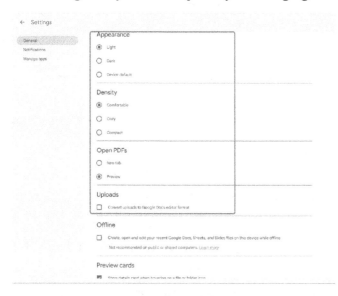

Integrating with Google's Ecosystem

The Home Screen connects seamlessly with other Google apps, allowing you to:

- Preview documents without leaving Drive.

- Launch files in Google Docs, Sheets, or Slides with a single click.

- Access recent emails with file attachments through the **Quick Access** area.

Common Issues and Fixes

Files Not Showing in Quick Access

Issue: Recently opened files don't appear in the Quick Access panel.
Solution:

1. Verify that Quick Access is enabled in settings.

2. Clear your browser cache or try accessing Drive in an incognito window to rule out browser-related issues.

Search Results Not Accurate

Issue: The search bar doesn't display the file you're looking for.
Solution:

1. Check if you're logged into the correct Google Account.

2. Use more specific search terms or filters.

3. Confirm that the file hasn't been deleted or moved to Trash.

Practical Exercises

To familiarize yourself with the Home Screen:

1. Open Google Drive and locate the search bar. Practice using filters like file type and owner.

2. Switch between List View and Grid View. Identify which view works better for different types of files.

3. Explore the Quick Access panel. Pin a file, then unpin it to understand the functionality.

Summary

The Home Screen is your starting point in Google Drive, designed to provide quick access to files, efficient search tools, and easy navigation. Mastering its layout and features will save you time and improve your productivity as you work in Google Drive. By learning how to use the search bar, customizing the interface, and resolving common issues, you're setting a strong foundation for effective file management.

1.3.2 Understanding the Sidebar

The sidebar in Google Drive serves as the central navigation hub, providing users with quick access to different areas of their Drive and essential functions. By mastering the sidebar, users can streamline their workflow and find what they need efficiently. This section will provide a comprehensive overview of the sidebar, breaking down its components and their uses.

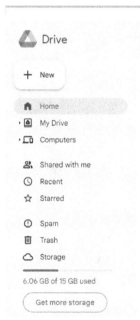

Overview of the Sidebar

The sidebar is located on the left-hand side of the Google Drive interface. It features a clean and intuitive design, with icons and labels organized vertically. Each section in the sidebar corresponds to a specific function or view within Google Drive. These sections include:

1. **My Drive**

2. **Shared with Me**

3. **Recent**

4. **Starred**

5. **Trash**

6. **Storage**

7. Additional options such as **Priority** and shortcuts to **Shared Drives** (if applicable).

Key Sections of the Sidebar

1. My Drive

This is the main area where all your personal files and folders are stored. When you click on "My Drive," you can:

- **View all your uploaded and created files.**
- **Organize your files into folders.**
- **Drag and drop files between locations.**

The **My Drive** section serves as the central repository for your Google Drive experience. All files created with Google Docs, Sheets, or Slides automatically save here unless directed otherwise.

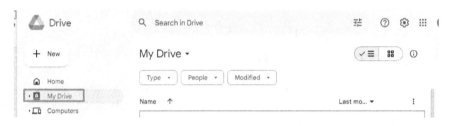

---

2. Shared with Me

This section displays files and folders shared by others. It is particularly useful for collaborative projects and team workspaces. Features include:

- Viewing a list of files shared by others, sorted by the most recent activity.
- **Searching within shared files** using the search bar.
- Identifying **ownership and permission levels** (e.g., "View only," "Edit").

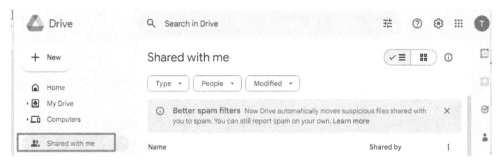

Tip: Files in this section are not automatically added to "My Drive." If you want quicker access, right-click a shared file and select **"Add shortcut to Drive."**

3. Recent

The Recent section is a time-saving tool that shows the most recently opened or modified files. Key benefits include:

- Quickly resuming work on your most recent files.

- Tracking changes or updates made by collaborators.

- Filtering by specific file types, such as Google Docs or PDFs.

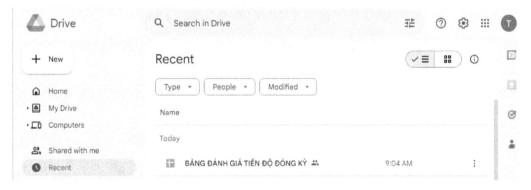

4. Starred

This section works like a "favorites" folder, allowing you to mark frequently accessed files and folders for easy retrieval. Features include:

- Marking files as "Starred" by right-clicking and selecting the **"Add to Starred"** option.

- Organizing your Starred items to create a curated list of high-priority files.

Pro Tip: Use the Starred section to keep track of files you need for upcoming meetings or deadlines.

---

5. Trash

The Trash section is where deleted files are stored temporarily. Key details include:

- Files in Trash remain for **30 days** before permanent deletion.

- You can manually delete files immediately by selecting **"Delete Forever."**

- Files can also be restored to their original location if deleted accidentally.

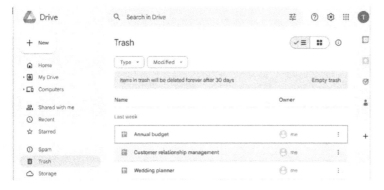

Warning: Deleted files no longer shared with collaborators unless restored.

---

6. Storage

At the bottom of the sidebar, the Storage section displays your current Google Drive usage. Information provided includes:

- The amount of space used vs. total available (e.g., 3 GB of 15 GB).

- A breakdown of file types taking up storage.

- The option to **upgrade storage plans** by clicking the "Buy storage" link.

Managing Storage Effectively:

- Use the Storage section to identify large files.

- Delete files no longer needed or move them to an external backup.

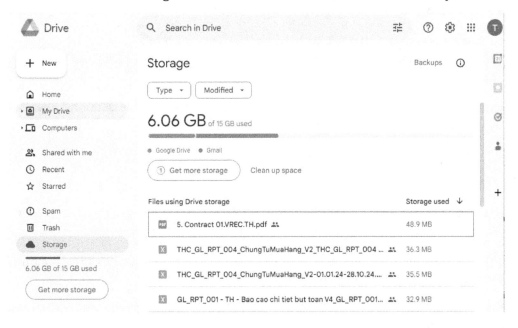

Additional Sidebar Features

Priority (if available)

The Priority section uses machine learning to predict and highlight files you might need based on recent activity. Features include:

- Suggested files and folders for quick access.

- Shortcuts to active collaboration workspaces.

Shared Drives

For Google Workspace users, the Shared Drives section provides access to team-based drives. Unlike "Shared with Me," Shared Drives are structured and collectively owned by the organization.

Customizing the Sidebar

Google Drive allows limited customization of the sidebar to suit your preferences:

1. **Reorganizing Items:** Drag sections like "Starred" or "Recent" higher for easier access.

2. **Hiding Sections:** Right-click on sections such as "Shared Drives" to hide them temporarily.

3. **Expanding/Collapsing Menus:** Click the small arrow beside sections like "My Drive" to expand or collapse nested folders.

Tips for Using the Sidebar Effectively

1. **Use the Search Bar:** Located at the top of the interface, the search bar can refine results across specific sections of the sidebar, saving time when locating files.

2. **Shortcut Commands:** Memorize common sidebar actions, such as pressing **Shift + Z** to add shortcuts to folders.

3. **Keep Organized:** Regularly review your My Drive, Shared with Me, and Trash sections to declutter and improve accessibility.

4. **Leverage Starred Files:** Make it a habit to star essential files for easy retrieval, especially during busy projects.

5. **Monitor Storage Usage:** Periodically check the Storage section to ensure you have adequate space for new uploads.

Common Challenges with the Sidebar

While the sidebar is intuitive, users may encounter minor challenges, such as:

- Difficulty locating shared files among a large volume of content.

- Accidental deletion of files when organizing.

- Forgetting to manage storage until nearing the limit.

Solutions:

- Regularly clean up your Shared with Me section by adding shortcuts to frequently used files.

- Use the Trash section as a safety net for recovering lost data.

- Explore third-party tools like Google Workspace Add-ons for enhanced organization.

By understanding the components of the sidebar and using its features effectively, users can significantly enhance their Google Drive experience. Whether you are managing personal documents or collaborating on team projects, the sidebar is your key to a more organized and efficient workflow.

1.3.3 Key Menu Options

The **menu options** in Google Drive are the core tools that allow users to perform essential tasks like organizing, creating, and sharing files. Whether you're a beginner or someone looking to streamline your workflow, understanding these key options will empower you to make the most of this cloud-based platform.

Overview of Key Menu Options

When you open Google Drive, you'll notice a navigation bar on the left and several menu options available at the top of the screen. Each of these menus serves a unique purpose, allowing you to interact with your files efficiently. Below is a breakdown of these menus and their functionalities.

1. New Button

Located in the upper-left corner, the **New** button is your starting point for creating and uploading files.

- **Create New Files**: Clicking this button allows you to create Google Docs, Sheets, Slides, and other types of files.

    o *Google Docs*: For text documents like reports or letters.

    o *Google Sheets*: For spreadsheets and data analysis.

    o *Google Slides*: For presentations and slideshows.

- **Upload Files or Folders**: You can upload files or entire folders from your computer. This feature is especially helpful when transitioning files to the cloud.

- **Integration with Other Apps**: Depending on your setup, you may see third-party apps like Google Forms or Jamboard available here.

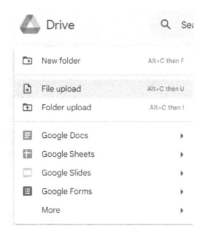

2. My Drive

The **My Drive** section is the primary space where your files and folders are stored.

- **Organize Files**: Use this space to create folders, rearrange files, or categorize them with color codes.

- **Drag-and-Drop Functionality**: Files can be easily moved within this section by dragging and dropping them into folders.

- **Customization**: Right-click on items to see options like renaming, sharing, or downloading.

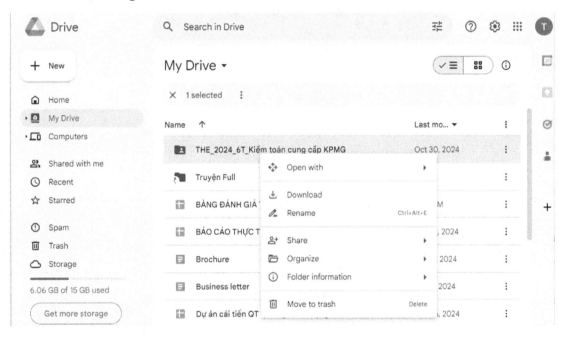

3. Shared with Me

The **Shared with Me** menu lists files and folders that others have shared with you.

- **Viewing Shared Content**: Files are organized chronologically, with the most recent at the top.

- **Understanding Permissions**: The icons here indicate whether you can view, comment, or edit a file.

- **Organizing Shared Files**: While you cannot move shared files into your My Drive directly, you can add shortcuts for easier access.

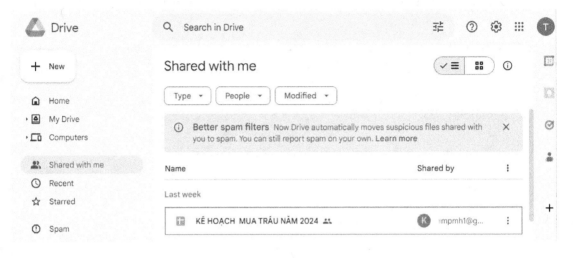

4. Recent

The **Recent** menu is a handy feature for accessing files you've worked on or viewed recently.

- **Quick Access**: Files are sorted based on the last opened or modified date.

- **Efficient Workflow**: This is particularly useful for accessing files during active projects without having to search for them.

5. Starred

The **Starred** section helps you bookmark files and folders that are important or frequently accessed.

- **Adding Stars**: Right-click a file or folder and select "Add to Starred."

- **Organized Favorites**: Starred files appear in this section, making them easy to locate.

- **Use Cases**: Ideal for critical documents like contracts, presentations, or ongoing work.

6. Trash

The **Trash** menu holds files and folders you've deleted, providing an opportunity for recovery if needed.

- **Storage Duration**: Deleted items remain in the Trash for 30 days before being permanently removed.

- **Restoring Items**: Right-click on a file in Trash and select "Restore" to recover it.

- **Permanently Delete**: You can manually empty the Trash to free up storage space.

7. Search Bar

Although not a menu item, the **Search Bar** is an essential navigation tool located at the top of the screen.

- **Keyword Search**: Enter file names, file types, or keywords to find specific documents.

- **Filters**: Use filters like file type, date modified, or owner to refine your search.

- **Smart Suggestions**: Google Drive uses AI to suggest files you might be looking for.

8. Settings Menu

The **Settings Menu** (accessible via the gear icon) allows you to customize your Google Drive experience.

- **General Settings**: Manage default file formats, offline access, and notifications.

- **Storage Details**: Check how much space you're using and upgrade if needed.

- **Integrations**: Link other Google tools or third-party apps to streamline your workflow.

Using the Menus Effectively

Now that you understand the purpose of each menu, let's discuss how to use them effectively:

1. **Organize Regularly**: Spend time organizing files in My Drive using folders and labels. This will make finding files quicker and easier.

2. **Leverage Shortcuts**: Use the Starred section to keep your most-used files just a click away.

3. **Clean Up**: Regularly review the Trash and delete unnecessary files to free up space.

4. **Search Smartly**: Use advanced search options to locate files faster, especially in large drives.

Practical Example: Managing a Project

Let's consider a scenario where you're managing a team project:

- **Step 1**: Create a folder in My Drive and name it "Project XYZ."

- **Step 2**: Use the New button to create subfolders for "Documents," "Presentations," and "Data."

- **Step 3**: Share the folder with team members via the Shared with Me menu and set appropriate permissions.

- **Step 4**: Bookmark critical files using the Starred menu for quick access during meetings.

Conclusion

Mastering the key menu options in Google Drive is fundamental to becoming an efficient user. These tools are designed to enhance your productivity by making file management intuitive and seamless. By understanding and utilizing these menus effectively, you'll unlock the full potential of Google Drive and streamline your workflow like a pro.

CHAPTER II
Creating and Uploading Files

2.1 Creating New Files

2.1.1 Google Docs

Google Docs is one of the most versatile and widely used tools within Google Drive. It is a web-based word processor that allows users to create, edit, and collaborate on text documents in real-time. Whether you're writing an essay, drafting a report, or creating meeting minutes, Google Docs offers a user-friendly platform for all your text-based needs.

Getting Started with Google Docs

To create a new Google Docs file:

1.   Open Google Drive.

2.   Click on the **"+ New"** button in the upper-left corner.

3.   From the dropdown menu, select **"Google Docs"**.

4.   A new tab will open, displaying a blank document titled **"Untitled Document"**.

You can immediately start typing or customize the title by clicking on it in the top-left corner.

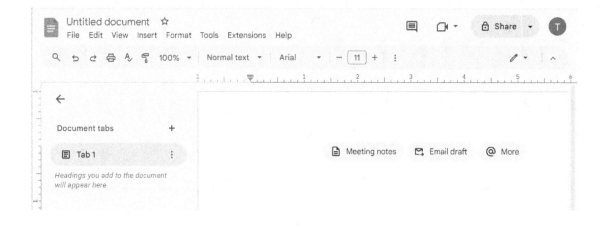

Navigating the Google Docs Interface

The Google Docs interface is intuitive and streamlined, designed to mimic traditional word processors while adding unique online collaboration features.

Key Sections:

- **Toolbar**: The toolbar at the top provides access to formatting tools, font styles, text alignment, and more.

- **File Menu**: The top menu contains options like File, Edit, View, Insert, Format, and Tools.

- **Document Body**: The main workspace where you create and edit text.

Core Features and Their Applications

Text Formatting

Google Docs provides a robust set of formatting options:

- **Font Selection and Size**: Choose from dozens of font styles and adjust sizes for emphasis.

- **Bold, Italic, and Underline**: Use these features to highlight important sections of your text.

- **Text Color and Highlighting**: Add color to specific words or phrases to draw attention.

- **Alignment**: Adjust text alignment (left, center, right, or justified) to match document requirements.

Paragraph Styles

For structured documents, Google Docs allows you to apply headings and subheadings:

- Use **Heading 1**, **Heading 2**, etc., to create an organized hierarchy.

- This structure not only improves readability but also enables automatic Table of Contents generation.

Collaborating in Real-Time

One of Google Docs' standout features is its real-time collaboration capability.

- **Sharing**: Click the **"Share"** button in the top-right corner to invite others. Assign roles like Viewer, Commenter, or Editor.

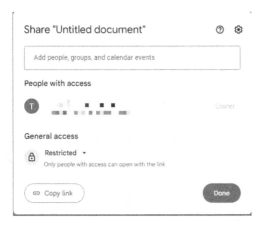

- **Live Edits**: Changes made by collaborators appear instantly, marked with their user icons.

- **Commenting**: Highlight text and click the comment icon to leave notes or suggestions.

- **Version History**: Track all edits via **File > Version History**, ensuring you never lose important changes.

Templates for Efficiency

Google Docs includes a variety of templates to save time and maintain professionalism.

- **Resume Templates**: Ideal for job seekers.
- **Business Letters**: Ready-made formats for official correspondence.
- **Project Proposals**: Pre-designed layouts to kickstart your project documentation.

Access templates by clicking **File > New > From Template Gallery**.

Inserting Elements into Your Document

Google Docs allows you to integrate multimedia and interactive elements seamlessly.

Images

- Insert images via **Insert > Image**. You can upload from your computer, search the web, or import directly from Google Photos.

Tables

- Organize data using tables. Go to **Insert > Table** and select the desired dimensions.

Links

- Add hyperlinks with **Ctrl + K** (or Command + K on Mac) to connect your document to external resources.

Charts and Diagrams

- Integrate charts directly from Google Sheets or create flowcharts with third-party add-ons.

Working Offline

Even though Google Docs is primarily cloud-based, it supports offline use.

- Enable offline mode through **Google Drive settings**.
- Work without an internet connection, and your changes will sync once you're back online.

Practical Use Cases of Google Docs

Academic Use

Students can create essays, research papers, and group projects efficiently.

- Collaborate with peers on the same document.

- Use **Explore** (in the bottom-right corner) for built-in research assistance.

Professional Use

Google Docs is ideal for drafting reports, meeting agendas, and proposals.

- **Sharing** ensures team input without endless email chains.
- Use **Comments and Suggestions** for feedback from managers or colleagues.

Personal Use

For personal tasks like journaling, planning events, or creating to-do lists, Google Docs is accessible and convenient.

Integrations and Extensions

Google Drive Integration

All Google Docs files are automatically stored in Google Drive, ensuring easy organization and access.

Third-Party Add-ons

Enhance functionality with add-ons like Grammarly (for grammar checking) or DocSecrets (for encrypted text). Access these via **Extensions > Add-ons > Get add-ons**.

Tips for Mastering Google Docs

1. **Use Keyboard Shortcuts**
   - For example, **Ctrl + B** for bold or **Ctrl + Shift + C** to word count.
2. **Leverage Voice Typing**
   - Activate through **Tools > Voice Typing** and dictate your content for hands-free writing.
3. **Explore Document Outline**
   - Use **View > Show Outline** to navigate large documents effortlessly.
4. **Embed Google Sheets**

o Integrate live spreadsheets into your document to display dynamic data.

Troubleshooting Common Issues

- **Slow Loading**: Clear browser cache or check internet speed.

- **Collaboration Conflicts**: Resolve through version history to review and merge changes.

- **Formatting Errors**: Use the **Clear Formatting** option to reset problematic text.

Conclusion

Mastering Google Docs is the first step toward unlocking the full potential of Google Drive. Its versatility, collaboration features, and seamless integration with other Google tools make it an indispensable resource for users of all skill levels.

2.1.2 Google Sheets

Google Sheets is one of the most versatile tools offered within the Google Workspace suite, allowing users to create and manage spreadsheets seamlessly in the cloud. Whether you're tracking budgets, analyzing data, or creating charts, Google Sheets provides a powerful, collaborative platform that rivals traditional spreadsheet software. In this section, we'll explore the key features of Google Sheets, how to create a new spreadsheet, and essential tips to get started.

What is Google Sheets?

Google Sheets is a web-based spreadsheet application that allows users to store data, perform calculations, and create visual representations of information. Because it is cloud-based, all changes are saved automatically in real-time, making it a perfect tool for collaboration and access from any device.

Key features of Google Sheets include:

- **Collaboration**: Multiple users can edit the same spreadsheet simultaneously.

- **Formulas and Functions**: Perform calculations, analyze data, and automate tasks using built-in functions.

- **Data Visualization**: Create charts, graphs, and pivot tables to summarize data effectively.

- **Integration**: Seamlessly connect with other Google apps like Google Docs, Slides, and Forms.

How to Create a New Spreadsheet

Creating a new spreadsheet in Google Sheets is simple. Follow these steps:

1. **Accessing Google Sheets**:

     o Open your web browser and navigate to Google Sheets. Alternatively, you can access it through Google Drive by clicking the "New" button and selecting **Google Sheets** from the dropdown menu.

2. **Starting from Scratch**:

     o Select the blank spreadsheet option labeled **Blank** to open a new, untitled spreadsheet.

3. **Using Templates**:

     o Google Sheets offers a range of pre-designed templates for tasks like budgeting, invoicing, and scheduling. Click **Template gallery** at the top of the main page to browse options and select one that suits your needs.

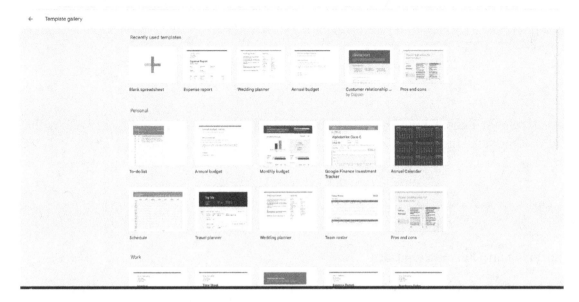

4. **Naming Your Spreadsheet**:

   o At the top-left corner, click **Untitled Spreadsheet** and type a descriptive name for your file. This name will help you locate it easily later in Google Drive.

Exploring the Interface

When you open a new Google Sheets file, you'll see several key components:

1. **Menu Bar**: Includes tabs like File, Edit, View, and Tools for accessing advanced options.

2. **Toolbar**: Contains shortcuts for common actions, such as formatting, inserting charts, and applying filters.

3. **Grid Area**: A matrix of rows and columns where you enter and manipulate data.

4. **Sheet Tabs**: Found at the bottom, allowing you to manage multiple sheets within the same file.

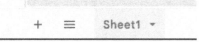

Entering and Formatting Data

Once your spreadsheet is ready, you can start inputting data:

1. **Adding Data**:

   o Click on any cell to select it and begin typing. Use the **Tab** key to move horizontally and the **Enter** key to move vertically.

2. **Formatting Data**:

   o Use the toolbar to apply formatting such as bold, italics, and text color. For numbers, you can adjust formats like currency, percentages, and dates.

Using Basic Formulas and Functions

Google Sheets comes equipped with a wide range of formulas to automate calculations. Here are a few basics:

- **SUM**: Adds a range of numbers. Example: =SUM(A1:A10)

- **AVERAGE**: Calculates the average of a range. Example: =AVERAGE(B1:B10)

- **IF**: Performs logical tests. Example: =IF(A1>10, "Yes", "No")

Collaboration and Sharing

One of the standout features of Google Sheets is the ability to collaborate in real-time:

1. **Sharing the File**:

   o   Click the **Share** button at the top-right corner. Enter email addresses and set permissions (Viewer, Commenter, or Editor).

2. **Real-Time Edits**:

   o   Changes made by collaborators appear instantly, with individual user cursors marked by colored indicators.

3. **Adding Comments**:

   o   Highlight a cell, right-click, and select **Comment** to leave notes or feedback for your collaborators.

Creating Charts and Visualizations

Google Sheets makes it easy to create visual representations of your data:

1. **Highlight Your Data**:

   o   Select the cells containing the data you want to visualize.

2. **Insert a Chart**:

   o   Click **Insert > Chart**. A default chart will appear, which you can customize through the Chart Editor.

3. **Customize Your Chart**:

   o   Change the chart type (e.g., bar, line, pie) and adjust colors, labels, and titles for clarity.

Tips for Beginners

- **Learn Shortcuts**: Familiarize yourself with keyboard shortcuts like Ctrl+C (Copy), Ctrl+V (Paste), and Ctrl+Z (Undo).

- **Use Conditional Formatting**: Highlight cells that meet specific criteria (e.g., values greater than 100) to make trends or anomalies stand out.

- **Explore Add-ons**: Extend the functionality of Google Sheets by installing add-ons like **Supermetrics** for data integration or **Power Tools** for advanced editing.

Practical Applications

Google Sheets is highly adaptable to various scenarios. Some common use cases include:

- **Personal Budgeting**: Track expenses and savings.

- **Team Project Management**: Use collaborative spreadsheets to assign tasks and monitor progress.

- **Data Analysis**: Use pivot tables and charts to uncover insights.

Conclusion

Mastering Google Sheets begins with understanding its basic functions and exploring its collaborative potential. With consistent practice, even beginners can unlock the full power of this versatile tool. Once you're comfortable with the fundamentals, you can explore advanced features to further enhance your productivity and efficiency.

This concludes **2.1.2 Google Sheets**. In the next section, we will dive into **2.1.3 Google Slides**, where you'll learn how to create compelling presentations directly within Google Drive.

2.1.3 Google Slides

Google Slides is a versatile tool for creating engaging presentations, whether for business, education, or personal use. It offers a user-friendly interface, collaborative features, and integration with other Google Workspace apps. This section will guide you through the process of creating a new Google Slides presentation, customizing it, and leveraging its powerful features.

What is Google Slides?

Google Slides is a cloud-based presentation software that allows you to design slideshows with ease. It supports text, images, videos, charts, and animations to create visually appealing and interactive presentations. The collaborative nature of Google Slides makes it an ideal choice for teams working together in real-time.

How to Create a New Google Slides Presentation

1. **Accessing Google Slides:**
   To create a new Google Slides file:

      o   Open Google Drive and click the **New** button in the upper-left corner.

      o   Select **Google Slides** from the dropdown menu. You can choose to start with a blank presentation or use one of the templates.

      o   Alternatively, navigate directly to Google Slides and click **Blank Presentation** or browse available templates.

2. **Choosing a Template:**
   Google Slides offers various pre-designed templates for different use cases, including business reports, lesson plans, and creative portfolios. Templates save time by providing a ready-made layout that you can customize.

3. **Naming Your Presentation:**
   Before you begin editing, click on the default file name at the top-left corner of the screen. Rename the file to reflect its purpose, e.g., "Marketing Plan 2024" or "Science Project Overview."

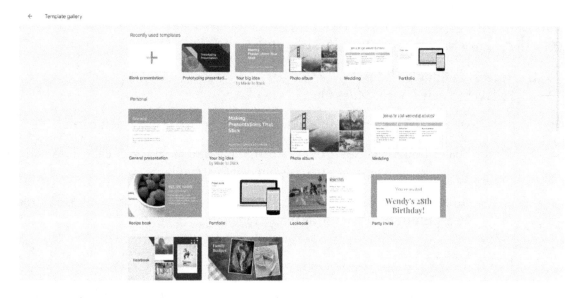

Navigating the Google Slides Interface

The Google Slides workspace is divided into three main sections:

- **Slide Navigation Pane:** Located on the left, this pane displays a thumbnail view of all slides in your presentation.

- **Main Slide Editor:** The center of the screen is where you edit the content of each slide.

- **Toolbar and Menu Bar:** At the top, you'll find tools for formatting text, adding shapes, inserting media, and managing slides.

Adding and Customizing Slides

1. **Adding a New Slide:**

   o Click the **+ (Add Slide)** button in the toolbar, or right-click in the Slide Navigation Pane and select **New Slide.**

   o Use the dropdown next to the **+** button to choose a specific slide layout, such as title-only, title-and-content, or a blank slide.

2. **Editing Slide Layouts:**

   o Double-click any placeholder text to edit titles, subtitles, or body text.

   o Resize or move elements by clicking and dragging their edges.

3. **Customizing Backgrounds:**

   o Right-click on the slide and select **Change Background.**

   o Choose a solid color, gradient, or upload an image to personalize the slide background.

Inserting Content into Slides

Google Slides supports a variety of content types to make presentations dynamic and engaging:

1. **Text:**
   - Click **Insert > Text Box** or use the toolbar's Text Box button to add text anywhere on the slide.
   - Format text using font styles, sizes, colors, and alignment options.

2. **Images:**
   - Select **Insert > Image** to upload pictures from your device, search the web, or insert from Google Photos.
   - Resize and reposition images using the drag handles.

3. **Videos:**
   - Click **Insert > Video** and paste a YouTube URL or select a video from Google Drive.
   - Customize playback options like autoplay or loop.

4. **Shapes and Lines:**
   - Use **Insert > Shape** or **Insert > Line** to add visual elements like arrows, rectangles, or connectors.

5. **Charts and Tables:**
   - Import data visualizations by selecting **Insert > Chart** or **Table.**
   - Link charts from Google Sheets for dynamic updates.

Working with Themes and Master Slides

1. **Applying a Theme:**
   - Click **Theme** in the toolbar to choose from pre-designed color schemes and layouts.
   - Themes ensure consistent design across all slides.

2. **Customizing Master Slides:**

- o Access **Slide > Edit Master** to modify the overall layout, fonts, and placeholders for the entire presentation.

- o Changes made to the master slide reflect across all slides using that layout.

Collaboration Features in Google Slides

1. **Sharing the Presentation:**

   - o Click the **Share** button in the top-right corner. Add collaborators using their email addresses and set permissions (Viewer, Commenter, Editor).

   - o Generate a shareable link for broader distribution.

2. **Real-Time Collaboration:**

   - o Team members can edit the presentation simultaneously.

   - o Use the **Comments** feature to leave feedback or suggestions.

3. **Revision History:**

   - o Access **File > Version History > See Version History** to view and restore previous edits.

Presenting with Google Slides

1. **Presentation Mode:**

   - o Click the **Present** button to display your slides in full-screen mode. Use the arrow keys to navigate between slides.

2. **Presenter View:**

   - o Use Presenter View to see your notes while projecting the slides to an audience.

   - o Access additional tools like a timer and Q&A during the presentation.

3. **Sharing a Link to Present:**

   - o Generate a presentation-specific link that automatically starts in Present mode.

Pro Tips for Effective Slideshows

- **Keep it Simple:** Limit text and focus on visuals to make your slides easy to follow.

- **Use High-Quality Images:** Avoid pixelated or low-resolution pictures.

- **Follow a Consistent Theme:** Use the same fonts, colors, and styles across all slides.

- **Practice Presenting:** Familiarize yourself with the flow and timing of your presentation.

By mastering Google Slides, you can create stunning presentations that communicate your ideas effectively, whether you're in the boardroom, the classroom, or hosting a webinar. Continue exploring additional tools and techniques to elevate your presentation skills.

2.2 Uploading Files and Folders

2.2.1 Supported File Types

Google Drive supports a wide range of file types, making it a versatile tool for storing and managing almost any kind of document, media, or data. Understanding which file types are supported and how they interact with Google Drive can help you make the most of its features.

Overview of Supported File Types

Google Drive is designed to handle a variety of file types, categorized into the following groups:

1. **Document Files**:

   o Google Drive fully supports common document formats like **.docx** (Microsoft Word), **.odt** (OpenDocument Text), and **.rtf** (Rich Text Format).

   o Native Google file formats, such as **Google Docs**, are also supported and optimized for collaboration.

   o Other text-based formats like **.txt** are easily uploadable and viewable directly in Drive.

2. **Spreadsheet Files**:

   o Files like **.xlsx** (Microsoft Excel), **.ods** (OpenDocument Spreadsheet), and **Google Sheets** are fully compatible.

   o These files can be opened, edited, and saved back to their original formats or converted into Google Sheets for easier editing and sharing.

3. **Presentation Files**:

   o Google Drive supports **.pptx** (Microsoft PowerPoint), **.odp** (OpenDocument Presentation), and its native **Google Slides** format.

   o These files can be imported and viewed seamlessly within the platform.

4. **Image Files**:

- o Common image formats such as **.jpeg**, **.png**, **.gif**, **.bmp**, **.svg**, and **.tiff** can be uploaded.

- o Google Drive also supports editing and viewing some image files through connected apps or Google Photos integration.

5. **Audio Files**:

- o Audio formats like **.mp3**, **.wav**, and **.ogg** are supported for storage and playback directly in Google Drive.

- o These files can also be shared with collaborators or linked to Google Slides presentations.

6. **Video Files**:

- o Popular formats such as **.mp4, .avi, .mov, .wmv**, and **.mkv** are uploadable.

- o Google Drive provides a built-in video player for instant playback without the need for additional software.

7. **Compressed Files**:

- o Compressed files like **.zip** and **.rar** are supported and can be downloaded or opened using third-party tools integrated with Google Drive.

8. **Specialized File Types**:

- o Files such as **PDFs**, **vector graphics (.eps)**, and even coding files like **HTML**, **CSS**, and **JavaScript** can be stored and accessed.

- o Google Drive also works with files created by specialized software like AutoCAD (.dwg) when appropriate apps are integrated.

Converting Files to Google Formats

One of the standout features of Google Drive is its ability to convert certain file types into Google's native formats (Google Docs, Sheets, and Slides). This allows users to edit, share, and collaborate on files in real-time.

- **Supported Conversions**:

- o Microsoft Office files (**.docx, .xlsx, .pptx**) can be converted into their respective Google formats.

- o PDF files can be partially converted into editable Google Docs if they contain text that Google Drive can recognize.

- **How to Convert**:

  - o Upon uploading, Google Drive may prompt you to convert the file. You can also enable automatic conversion by adjusting your Drive settings:

    1. Navigate to **Settings** in Google Drive.

    2. Enable the option **"Convert uploaded files to Google Docs editor format."**

Unsupported File Types and Workarounds

While Google Drive supports a wide range of file types, some specialized files may not be directly viewable or editable within the platform. Examples include:

- Executable files like **.exe** or **.bat**, which are restricted for security reasons.

- Certain proprietary formats used by niche software applications.

To work around these limitations, you can:

- **Store files for download**: Unsupported file types can still be stored safely in Google Drive and downloaded when needed.

- **Use third-party apps**: Many unsupported file types can be opened with integrated apps from the Google Workspace Marketplace.

Maximizing Compatibility

To ensure smooth usage across devices and platforms:

1. Stick to widely used formats like **PDF**, **JPEG**, or **MP4**, which are universally supported.

2. Convert files to Google formats whenever possible for enhanced functionality and collaboration.

3. Keep software up-to-date to avoid issues with file compatibility when importing or exporting.

Storage Limits for File Types

Google Drive provides generous storage allowances, but individual files have size limits:

- Documents: Up to **50 MB** for text files converted to Google Docs.

- Spreadsheets: Up to **5 million cells** for Google Sheets.

- Presentations: Up to **100 MB** for Google Slides files.

- Other file types: Files up to **5 TB** can be uploaded as long as your account has sufficient storage space.

Practical Tips for Managing File Types

1. **Organize files by type**: Use folders and consistent naming conventions to group files for easier access.

2. **Preview before downloading**: Google Drive's preview function allows you to view files without fully downloading them.

3. **Check sharing permissions**: Ensure collaborators can open files by setting permissions compatible with the file format.

By understanding the range of file types supported by Google Drive, you can unlock its full potential as a versatile and user-friendly cloud storage solution. Whether you're working with text documents, media files, or specialized formats, Google Drive provides the tools to store, manage, and collaborate efficiently.

2.2.2 Drag-and-Drop Uploads

Google Drive's drag-and-drop functionality is one of its most user-friendly features. It allows users to upload files and folders effortlessly by simply dragging them from their computer into the Google Drive interface. This section explores how to make the most of drag-and-drop uploads, tips for organizing files during the upload process, and common troubleshooting scenarios.

How to Use Drag-and-Drop for File Uploads

Uploading files with drag-and-drop is straightforward and intuitive. Follow these simple steps to get started:

1. **Open Google Drive**

   Navigate to Google Drive and ensure you are logged into your Google account. If you are using the desktop version, you will see a clean interface with your current files and folders.

2. **Locate the Files on Your Computer**
   Open the file explorer (Windows) or Finder (Mac) on your computer. Locate the files or folders you want to upload to Google Drive.

3. **Drag and Drop**

   Click and hold the file or folder with your mouse, drag it to the Google Drive browser window, and release it. A blue overlay will appear on the Google Drive interface, indicating the drop zone.

4. **Upload Confirmation**

   Once the file or folder is dropped, Google Drive will begin the upload process. A progress bar will appear in the bottom-right corner of your screen, showing upload progress.

Advantages of Drag-and-Drop Uploads

- **Ease of Use**: Drag-and-drop eliminates the need to navigate through menus, making it perfect for beginners.

- **Batch Uploads**: Multiple files and folders can be uploaded at once, streamlining the process.

- **Time Efficiency**: This method is quick, especially when uploading files directly to a specific folder.

- **Organization During Uploads**: You can choose the exact location in your Google Drive where the files will be stored before starting the upload.

Best Practices for Drag-and-Drop Uploads

1. **Organize Files Before Uploading**
   Before initiating a drag-and-drop upload, ensure that your files are named appropriately and organized into folders. This will save time and effort when searching for files later.

2. **Select the Right Folder**
   Navigate to the specific folder in Google Drive where you want to store your files before dragging and dropping them. This helps maintain an organized Drive and reduces the need to move files later.

3. **Verify Upload Completion**

   After uploading, double-check that all files and folders were uploaded successfully. Occasionally, larger files might encounter issues, so it's good practice to confirm their presence.

4. **Use Chrome for Optimal Performance**
   While drag-and-drop works in most browsers, Google Chrome is optimized for Google Drive, ensuring smoother uploads and fewer interruptions.

5. **Ensure Stable Internet Connection**
   A stable internet connection is crucial for seamless uploads. If you're uploading large files, interruptions in the connection can lead to incomplete uploads.

Organizing Files During Drag-and-Drop

One key advantage of drag-and-drop uploads is the ability to organize files directly. Here's how you can enhance your file organization during the process:

- **Dragging into Subfolders**: If your Google Drive contains nested folders, you can drag files directly into these subfolders. This minimizes manual file movement after the upload.

- **Creating New Folders**: Right-click in Google Drive and select "New Folder" before starting the drag-and-drop process. This ensures your files are categorized from the start.

- **Using Starred Items**: For files that require immediate attention, you can star them after upload for quick access.

Common Challenges and Troubleshooting

Although drag-and-drop uploads are simple, users may occasionally encounter challenges. Here's how to address common issues:

1. **File Not Uploading**

   o **Cause**: This may occur due to unsupported file types or size limitations.

   o **Solution**: Check Google Drive's file upload limits and ensure your file type is supported. Split large files into smaller parts if necessary.

2. **Upload Interrupted**

   o **Cause**: A weak or unstable internet connection can disrupt uploads.

   o **Solution**: Retry the upload once your connection stabilizes. If the issue persists, use Google Drive's manual upload feature.

3. **Files Missing After Upload**

   o **Cause**: Files might not upload to the intended folder.

   o **Solution**: Use Google Drive's search bar to locate recently uploaded files.

4. **Browser Compatibility Issues**

   o **Cause**: Certain browsers may not fully support drag-and-drop functionality.

    o   **Solution**: Switch to Google Chrome for the best experience.

Tips for Dragging and Dropping Folders

Google Drive also allows entire folders to be uploaded using drag-and-drop. This feature is particularly useful for users managing projects with multiple files. Here are some tips:

- **Compress Large Folders**: If you're uploading a folder with hundreds of files, consider compressing it into a .zip file to ensure quicker uploads.

- **Folder Nesting**: Ensure that folder structures are logical and consistent. For example, use subfolders for documents, images, and videos within a main project folder.

- **Preview Uploaded Folders**: Once a folder is uploaded, navigate through its contents in Google Drive to ensure all files are intact.

Use Cases for Drag-and-Drop Uploads

- **Personal Projects**: Quickly upload vacation photos or personal documents for easy access across devices.

- **Workplace Collaboration**: Upload large datasets or shared resources into team folders effortlessly.

- **Education**: Teachers and students can organize and upload class materials, assignments, and multimedia files.

Conclusion

The drag-and-drop feature in Google Drive combines simplicity with efficiency, making it a go-to method for both new and experienced users. By mastering this functionality, you can save time, reduce frustration, and keep your Drive well-organized. Always remember to verify uploads and use stable internet for optimal results. With practice, drag-and-drop uploads will become second nature in your daily workflow.

2.2.3 Using the Upload Button

The Upload Button is one of the most straightforward tools in Google Drive for adding files and folders to your cloud storage. Whether you're a beginner or an experienced user, mastering this feature will significantly improve your ability to manage and organize your files. This section explores the process of using the Upload Button in detail, along with tips to make your workflow efficient and effective.

Locating the Upload Button

The Upload Button is located prominently within the Google Drive interface. You can find it in the top-left corner of the Google Drive home screen, next to the **New** button. Clicking the **New** button reveals a dropdown menu that provides access to several key options, including file and folder uploads.

- **File Upload:** Use this option to upload individual files from your local device to Google Drive.

- **Folder Upload:** Use this to upload entire folders, preserving their internal structure.

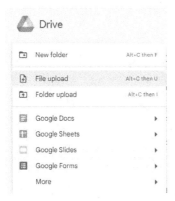

By understanding these options, you can decide whether you need to upload a single file or a collection of related files stored within a folder.

Step-by-Step Guide to Uploading Files

Step 1: Open Google Drive

Begin by navigating to the Google Drive website or opening the Google Drive app on your device. Ensure you are logged into your Google account.

Step 2: Click the New Button

Once on the home screen, click the **New** button located in the upper-left corner. This will open the dropdown menu, where you'll see the upload options.

Step 3: Select File Upload

Choose **File Upload** from the dropdown menu. A file explorer window will open, allowing you to browse your local device for the file you want to upload.

Step 4: Choose the File

Navigate to the location of your file, select it, and click **Open** (or the equivalent button in your operating system). Google Drive will begin uploading the file immediately.

Step 5: Monitor the Upload Process

As the file uploads, you'll see a progress bar at the bottom-right corner of your screen. This bar indicates the upload status, including time remaining and upload speed.

Uploading Folders with the Upload Button

Uploading folders is similar to uploading files but offers a more efficient way to handle multiple documents at once.

Step 1: Select Folder Upload

Click **New**, then choose **Folder Upload** from the dropdown menu.

Step 2: Locate the Folder

A file explorer window will appear. Navigate to the folder you want to upload, select it, and confirm your choice by clicking **Upload**.

Step 3: Confirm Folder Structure

Google Drive will upload the folder, including all subfolders and files within it. The folder's original structure will remain intact, ensuring you don't need to reorganize your files after the upload.

Key Features of the Upload Button

1. **Multiple File Selection:**
   You can upload multiple files at once by selecting them in the file explorer before clicking **Open**.

2. **Drag-and-Drop Compatibility:**

   While this section focuses on the Upload Button, it's worth noting that Google Drive supports drag-and-drop uploads. Simply drag your files or folders onto the Google Drive interface, and they will be uploaded automatically.

3. **Real-Time Notifications:**
   The progress bar keeps you updated on upload status, helping you monitor large files or batch uploads.

4. **Automatic Conversion:**

   If you upload files in formats like Microsoft Word or Excel, Google Drive can automatically convert them to Google Docs or Sheets formats. This setting can be enabled or disabled in the Drive settings menu.

Common Challenges and How to Overcome Them

1. **Slow Upload Speeds:**

   o **Cause:** Poor internet connectivity.

   o **Solution:** Check your connection, reduce bandwidth usage on other devices, or try uploading during off-peak hours.

2. **File Size Limits:**

   o **Cause:** Google Drive has a maximum file size limit (up to 5 TB for individual files).

   o **Solution:** Compress large files or split them into smaller parts if possible.

3. **Interrupted Uploads:**

   o **Cause:** Network interruptions.

   o **Solution:** Google Drive automatically resumes uploads when the connection is restored. However, ensure your device remains powered on during the process.

4. **Unsupported File Types:**

   o **Cause:** Some file types may not be supported for preview within Drive.

   o **Solution:** Upload the file as-is, then use an external program to view it, or convert it to a compatible format.

Optimizing Your Upload Process

1. **Organize Before Uploading:**

   To save time, organize your files and folders on your local device before uploading. This ensures your Drive remains tidy and well-structured.

2. **Set Permissions Immediately:**

   After uploading, right-click the file or folder and set sharing permissions to determine who can view or edit the content.

3. **Enable Offline Access:**

   If you plan to access your files without an internet connection, enable offline access for frequently used documents.

4. **Sync Large Files:**

   For extremely large files or frequent uploads, consider using the Google Drive desktop app. This tool allows seamless syncing between your local device and Drive.

Practical Scenarios for Using the Upload Button

1. **Student Projects:**

   Upload essays, presentations, and research materials for easy access and collaboration with classmates.

2. **Workplace Collaboration:**

   Share project files with team members or clients, ensuring everyone has the latest version.

3. **Personal Organization:**
   Store important personal documents, such as scanned receipts, contracts, and certificates, in a secure, easily accessible location.

4. **Backup and Recovery:**
   Use the Upload Button to back up critical files from your local device, ensuring they are safe even if your device fails.

By mastering the Upload Button, you unlock a powerful way to manage your files in Google Drive. It's simple, intuitive, and effective, making it an essential tool for users of all levels.

CHAPTER III
Organizing Your Drive

3.1 Creating and Managing Folders

3.1.1 Best Practices for Folder Organization

Organizing your Google Drive effectively is essential for maintaining productivity and reducing frustration when locating files. A well-structured folder system not only makes it easier to find documents but also ensures that your workflow remains efficient. In this section, we'll explore best practices for folder organization, offering tips and strategies to help you design a system that works for you.

Why Organizing Matters

Imagine opening your Google Drive and being greeted with a sea of files scattered chaotically across the interface. This kind of disarray can cost you precious time, lead to misplacing important documents, and even result in unnecessary duplication of work. A clear, logical folder structure prevents these problems, ensuring that you can focus on your tasks rather than searching for files.

1. Understand Your Needs

Before creating folders, consider the nature of your work and the types of files you use most frequently. For example:

- **Personal Users:** You might need folders for photos, financial documents, or hobby-related files.

- **Students:** Folders could be organized by courses, assignments, or extracurricular activities.

- **Professionals:** Categorize folders by projects, clients, or departments.

Take a moment to reflect on your specific needs. The clearer your understanding, the easier it will be to establish a functional folder system.

2. Use a Hierarchical Structure

A hierarchical folder structure is key to staying organized. Start with broad categories and create subfolders as needed. For example:

- **Main Folder:** Work
  - **Subfolder:** Client A
    - **Sub-subfolder:** Invoices
    - **Sub-subfolder:** Presentations
  - **Subfolder:** Client B

The goal is to create a "tree" structure where every file has a logical place, making navigation intuitive and straightforward.

3. Naming Conventions

Consistent and descriptive naming conventions are vital. Use clear, concise names that reflect the folder's content. Examples include:

- Use dates for time-sensitive projects: 2024_TaxDocuments.

- Use client or project names: Client_JohnsonProposal.

- Avoid ambiguous names like "Stuff" or "Miscellaneous."

Additionally, consider whether numbering folders (e.g., 01_ProjectName, 02_ClientFiles) would help maintain order. Alphabetical or chronological systems can add an extra layer of clarity.

4. Group Similar Items

Avoid scattering related files across multiple folders. For instance, if you're working on a project with multiple components (e.g., contracts, presentations, and meeting notes), group all these files under a single project folder.

Example:

- **Main Folder:** Marketing Campaign

    o **Subfolder:** Social Media

    o **Subfolder:** Budget

    o **Subfolder:** Reports

This approach minimizes the chances of files being overlooked or misplaced.

5. Regularly Review and Clean Up

A well-organized Drive requires occasional maintenance. Schedule periodic reviews to declutter and reorganize as necessary:

- **Archive Old Files:** Move outdated or inactive documents to an "Archive" folder.

- **Delete Unnecessary Files:** Clear out duplicates or files no longer relevant.

- **Reassess Folder Structure:** Adjust the hierarchy as your needs evolve.

6. Use Folder Color-Coding

Google Drive offers a handy feature for color-coding folders. Assigning colors to categories can make navigation faster and more intuitive. For example:

- **Blue:** Work-related folders

- **Green:** Personal finance

- **Yellow:** Creative projects

Color-coding is especially useful for users with a visual learning style, as it makes distinguishing folders at a glance easier.

7. Utilize Shared Folders

If you collaborate with others, shared folders can streamline the process. To keep shared folders organized:

- Clearly define the purpose of the folder.

- Use a naming convention that's clear to all participants.

- Restrict permissions appropriately to avoid accidental file edits or deletions.

8. Leverage Google Drive Search

While a robust folder system reduces the need for extensive searching, Google Drive's powerful search functionality is always there to back you up. Use search operators like type:pdf or owner:me to quickly locate specific files within your structured folders.

Practical Example: Implementing a Folder System

Scenario: You're a freelance graphic designer juggling multiple clients.

1. **Main Folders:** Create a folder for each client: Client_Alpha, Client_Beta, etc.

2. **Subfolders:** Within each client folder, create subfolders for Invoices, Design Drafts, and Final Deliverables.

3. **Naming Files:** Use descriptive names, such as 2024_LogoDesign_Final or 2023_Invoice_June.

4. **Color-Coding:** Assign a unique color to each client folder.

With this system, you'll always know where to find specific files related to each client.

Conclusion

Organizing your Google Drive with thoughtful folder structures and consistent practices pays off in the long run. By following these best practices, you'll not only save time but also reduce stress and increase efficiency. Remember, the key is to start with a simple structure and adapt it as your needs grow. With the right system in place, your Google Drive can become a powerful tool for personal and professional productivity.

3.1.2 Moving Files Between Folders

Moving files between folders in Google Drive is a fundamental skill that allows you to keep your workspace organized and efficient. Whether you're restructuring your folders, cleaning up duplicate files, or simply moving items to more appropriate locations, understanding how to manage files effectively ensures that your Google Drive remains a powerful tool for productivity. Below, we will explore step-by-step instructions, tips, and use cases for moving files between folders in Google Drive.

Why Move Files Between Folders?

There are many reasons to move files within Google Drive:

- **Improving Organization:** Shifting files to the correct folders ensures they are easier to locate in the future.

- **Decluttering Your Drive:** Consolidating files into fewer folders reduces clutter and enhances accessibility.

- **Streamlining Collaboration:** By placing files in shared folders, you ensure team members can access them without confusion.

- **Enhancing Workflow Efficiency:** Proper organization allows for seamless navigation and prevents wasted time searching for misplaced files.

Methods for Moving Files Between Folders

Google Drive provides multiple ways to move files between folders. Below are detailed guides for the most common methods:

1. Using Drag-and-Drop

One of the simplest ways to move files between folders is by dragging and dropping them:

1. **Open Google Drive**: Navigate to Google Drive and log in.

2. **Locate the File**: Find the file you want to move in the main view or search bar.

3. **Drag the File**: Click and hold the file, then drag it to the desired folder in the left-hand sidebar.

4. **Drop the File**: Release the mouse button to drop the file into the folder.

Tips for Drag-and-Drop:

- Ensure the target folder is visible in the sidebar before starting.

- Expand nested folders by clicking the small arrow next to a parent folder to drop files into subfolders.

- For multiple files, select them by holding down Ctrl (Windows) or Command (Mac) while clicking.

2. Using the "Move To" Option

This method is particularly useful if you prefer precision or are managing files on a smaller screen:

1. **Right-Click the File**: Find the file you want to move and right-click on it.

2. **Select "Move To"**: In the context menu, click on the "Move To" option.

3. **Choose a Folder**: A pop-up window will appear, showing your folder structure. Navigate to the desired folder.

4. **Click "Move Here"**: Once you've selected the correct folder, click the "Move Here" button to finalize.

Advantages of the "Move To" Option:

- Ensures accuracy when moving files deep within nested folder structures.

- Displays a clear overview of your Drive's folder organization.

- Reduces the risk of accidental drops compared to drag-and-drop.

3. Using the Keyboard Shortcut

For power users, keyboard shortcuts can significantly speed up the process:

1. **Select the File**: Click on the file you want to move.

2. **Press Shift + Z**: This opens the "Add to Folder" menu, where you can choose the target folder.

3. **Navigate and Confirm**: Use the arrow keys to select a folder and press Enter to move the file.

Note: The Shift + Z command can also be used to *add* a file to multiple folders without duplicating it.

4. Managing Files on Mobile Devices

If you're accessing Google Drive on a smartphone or tablet:

1. **Open the Google Drive App**: Download the app if you haven't already.

2. **Find the File**: Tap on the file you wish to move.

3. **Access the Options Menu**: Tap the three-dot menu icon next to the file.

4. **Select "Move"**: Choose the "Move" option, then navigate to the target folder.

5. **Confirm the Move**: Tap "Move Here" to complete the action.

Pro Tip for Mobile Users: Use the search bar to quickly locate files when working with large Drives.

Common Challenges When Moving Files

1. Moving Shared Files

Files shared with you can be added to your own Drive for better organization, but they may not always be moved freely depending on permissions. If you encounter issues, ensure you have edit access or request permission from the file owner.

2. Misplacing Files

Accidentally dropping files into the wrong folders can create confusion. Double-check the destination folder in the confirmation dialog to prevent misplacements.

3. Large Batch Transfers

When moving multiple files, processing times may vary depending on the number and size of files. For extensive transfers, break them into smaller batches for faster results.

Best Practices for Moving Files

- **Plan Your Folder Structure:** Create a logical folder hierarchy before moving files to avoid redundancy.

- **Use Naming Conventions:** Consistent file and folder names make it easier to locate items and confirm correct placement.

- **Review Shared Drives:** If you work collaboratively, ensure files are placed in shared folders where all team members can access them.

- **Set Up Quick Access Folders:** Pin frequently used folders to the sidebar for faster navigation.

Real-World Scenarios for Moving Files

1. **Team Collaboration:** A manager moves project files from their personal Drive to a shared folder for the entire team.

2. **Student Organization:** A student consolidates lecture notes from various courses into a semester-specific folder.

3. **Personal Archiving:** A user reorganizes family photos into year-based folders for easy retrieval.

Troubleshooting Moving Files

If you encounter difficulties while moving files:

- **Check Your Permissions:** Ensure you have edit access to both the file and the destination folder.

- **Clear Your Cache:** Browser issues can sometimes interfere with Drive functionality.

- **Contact Support:** Use Google's help resources for additional troubleshooting steps.

Mastering the process of moving files between folders empowers you to maintain an efficient and well-structured Google Drive. Whether you're handling a handful of personal files or managing an entire team's workspace, these techniques ensure that your Drive remains a valuable productivity tool. Take the time to experiment with different methods, and soon moving files will become second nature.

3.2 Using Stars and Color-Coding

Organizing files in Google Drive can seem overwhelming, especially when managing numerous documents, spreadsheets, and folders. However, two simple yet powerful features—**stars** and **color-coding**—make it easy to locate and prioritize files quickly. These tools allow you to visually differentiate important files and streamline your workflow.

What Are Stars in Google Drive?

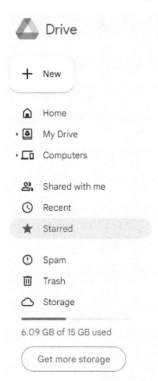

Stars in Google Drive are a way to bookmark or highlight files and folders for easy access. Think of them as a digital equivalent of adding a sticky note or flag to important documents. When you star a file, it becomes part of a dedicated "Starred" section in Google Drive, which you can access from the left-hand sidebar.

Benefits of Using Stars

• **Quick Access**: Starred files are easily accessible, eliminating the need to navigate through multiple folders.

• **Customizable**: You can decide which files or folders deserve a star, giving you control over what's prioritized.

• **Clutter-Free Workflow**: Starring keeps your "My Drive" uncluttered by grouping important items separately.

How to Star a File or Folder

1. Right-click on the file or folder you want to star.

2. Select **"Add to Starred"** from the dropdown menu.

3. Alternatively, open the file, click the star icon near the top of the interface.

To view your starred files, click **"Starred"** in the left-hand navigation bar.

Unstarring a File

If you no longer need a file to be starred, simply repeat the process and choose **"Remove from Starred."** This action will not delete the file; it simply removes the star designation.

Color-Coding Your Folders

Another excellent way to visually organize your Google Drive is by assigning colors to folders. By default, all folders are gray, but you can change their colors to signify categories, priorities, or themes.

Why Use Color-Coding?

1. **Visual Organization**: Color-coding makes it easy to distinguish folders at a glance. For instance, you might assign green for finance, blue for projects, and red for urgent matters.

2. **Improved Navigation**: When scanning through a crowded drive, colored folders stand out, helping you locate them faster.

3. **Enhanced Team Collaboration**: In shared drives, color-coding creates a consistent system for team members to follow.

How to Change Folder Colors

1. Right-click on the folder you want to color-code.

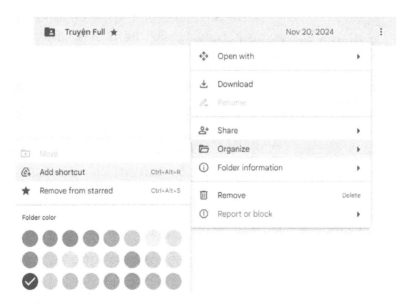

2. Hover over **"Change color"** in the dropdown menu.

3. Select a color from the palette provided.

4. The folder will instantly update to the chosen color.

Tips for Effective Color-Coding

- **Stick to a System**: Assign specific meanings to colors and use them consistently. For example:

    o   Red: Urgent tasks or high-priority projects

    o   Blue: Ongoing projects

    o   Yellow: Drafts or in-progress work

    o   Green: Completed work

- **Combine with Stars**: Use stars for individual files and colors for overarching categories.

Using Stars and Colors Together

Stars and color-coding complement each other. For example, you might color-code a folder for a specific project and star key files within it. This dual-layered organization helps you navigate both macro and micro levels of your work.

Example Use Case

Imagine you're managing a team project with multiple deliverables:

- The **main project folder** is colored **blue**.

- Subfolders for specific tasks, like **design**, **budgeting**, and **reporting**, are color-coded green, yellow, and purple, respectively.

- Important files, like the final report or design mockups, are starred for quick access.

This approach ensures that both you and your team can easily find what you need.

Practical Scenarios for Stars and Color-Coding

1. **Personal Projects**

   o   Use stars for frequently accessed files, such as resumes, budgets, or travel itineraries.

   o   Assign colors to distinguish personal, academic, or professional folders.

2. **Business and Team Collaboration**

   o   Star meeting agendas or critical documents to prepare for presentations.

   o   Color-code shared team folders by department or project phase.

3. **Student Use Case**

   o   Star lecture notes or assignment drafts.

   o   Use colors for different subjects or semesters.

Common Mistakes and How to Avoid Them

1. **Overusing Stars**

   Starring too many files defeats the purpose of prioritization. Be selective, reserving stars for truly important items.

2. **Inconsistent Color-Coding**

   Assigning random colors without a clear system can cause confusion. Stick to a predefined color scheme.

3. **Forgetting to Update**
   As projects progress, update your stars and colors to reflect current priorities.

Final Thoughts

Using stars and color-coding in Google Drive is a simple yet powerful way to enhance productivity. By combining these features strategically, you can create a system that keeps your files organized, accessible, and visually appealing. Take the time to experiment with these tools and develop a method that works best for your needs.

Next, we'll explore another crucial feature in Google Drive: Searching for Files.

3.3 Searching for Files

Efficiently locating files within Google Drive is a vital skill for staying organized and productive. Whether you are dealing with a vast repository of documents, spreadsheets, images, or other files, the ability to search and pinpoint what you need quickly can save significant time and effort. Google Drive's search functionality is robust, offering various options to tailor your searches and locate files effortlessly.

3.3.1 Search Filters

Google Drive includes a set of powerful search filters to help narrow down your results. These filters allow you to refine your search based on file type, owner, date modified, and other criteria. Below is a detailed explanation of how to use these filters effectively.

1. Accessing Search Filters

The search bar at the top of your Google Drive interface is your starting point. By clicking on the **filter icon** (a small funnel-shaped icon to the right of the search bar), you can open the advanced search options. Alternatively, you can type specific keywords directly into the search bar to trigger filter suggestions.

2. Types of Search Filters

Google Drive offers several filters to refine your search:

a. File Type

- Selecting the type of file you're searching for (e.g., documents, spreadsheets, presentations, PDFs) narrows down the results.

- Example: Searching for "marketing plan" and filtering by "Document" ensures you only see Google Docs files with that name.

b. Owner

- This filter helps identify whether you or someone else owns the file. You can search for files shared by specific individuals or files you own.

- Example: Looking for a file shared by your colleague? Select their name or email in the "Owner" dropdown.

c. Location

- Specify the folder or shared drive where the file might be stored.

- Example: Searching for a file located in "Team Projects" avoids searching through unrelated personal folders.

d. Date Modified

- This filter allows you to narrow your search by the timeframe of the last update. Options include today, the past week, the past month, or a custom date range.

- Example: Searching for files modified within the last month is ideal for finding recent projects.

e. File Name and Keywords

- Use the search bar to input specific file names or keywords. Keywords are particularly useful when you don't remember the exact name of a file but can recall some details.

- Example: Typing "budget Q1" brings up files containing those terms in their name or content.

f. Shared With

- This filter helps you find files that were shared with specific individuals.

- Example: If your manager shared a presentation, entering their email address in this filter will help locate it.

g. File Visibility

- Search for files based on their sharing settings, such as "Private," "Shared," or "Public."

- Example: Narrowing results to "Shared" ensures you only see files accessible to others.

3. Combining Filters

The true power of Google Drive's search filters lies in combining them to achieve highly specific results. For example:

- Searching for "report" with filters set to "PDF," "last modified in the past month," and "owned by me" retrieves only recent PDF reports you created.

- Filtering by a specific location and owner narrows your search within shared drives.

4. Boolean Operators for Advanced Search

For users familiar with advanced search techniques, Google Drive supports Boolean operators to enhance filtering:

- **AND**: Combine terms (e.g., "sales AND report") to find files containing both terms.

- **OR**: Retrieve files containing either term (e.g., "sales OR budget").

- **NOT**: Exclude specific terms (e.g., "report NOT draft").

- **Quotation Marks**: Search for exact phrases (e.g., "annual financial report").

Boolean operators can be used with filters to refine searches further.

5. Examples of Practical Use Cases

a. Finding Old Meeting Notes

Imagine you need to locate meeting notes from six months ago. Use the search bar with the keywords "meeting notes" and set the date modified filter to a custom range.

b. Locating a Presentation Shared by a Colleague

If a colleague named Sarah shared a presentation last week, search for "Sarah" in the owner filter and select "Presentation" in the file type filter.

c. Searching for Photos or Images

Google Drive allows you to find image files quickly by using the file type filter for "Images." Adding keywords such as "team event" can narrow it down further.

6. Tips for Effective Searching

- **Use Specific Keywords**: Avoid generic terms like "file" or "document," as they yield too many results.

- **Regularly Organize Files**: Well-organized folders and consistent naming conventions make searching easier.

- **Leverage Google's AI Suggestions**: As you type, Google Drive suggests results based on your activity. Take advantage of these smart suggestions.

- **Use Preview Mode**: Once you locate a file, click on it to preview its content without opening it fully. This saves time when verifying search results.

7. Limitations of Search Filters

While search filters in Google Drive are highly effective, there are some limitations to be aware of:

- Filters require accurate metadata. If a file isn't named or tagged effectively, it might be harder to locate.

- Searching large shared drives can take longer, especially with a high volume of files.

By mastering search filters in Google Drive, users can significantly reduce the time spent hunting for files. The combination of robust filters, Boolean operators, and AI suggestions ensures that you'll always find what you're looking for with minimal effort.

Examples to Illustrate the Use of Search Filters

Example 1: Finding a Report You Created Last Month

Let's say you need to locate a sales report you created in October. Follow these steps:

1. Go to the **Google Drive search bar** and click on the **filter icon**.

2. Under the **File type** dropdown, select **Documents**.

3. Set the **Owner** filter to **Owned by me**.

4. In the **Date modified** filter, choose **Custom date range** and set it to October 1 to October 31.

5. Type "Sales Report" into the search bar.

Result: Google Drive displays all documents containing "Sales Report" in their titles or content, created by you in October.

Example 2: Locating a Presentation Shared by a Team Member

Suppose your colleague Alex shared a presentation last week about marketing strategies. Here's how to find it:

1. Open the search bar and click on the **filter icon**.

2. Under **Owner**, type **Alex's email address** or select their name from the dropdown.

3. Choose **Presentation** from the **File type** filter.

4. Set the **Date modified** filter to **Last 7 days**.

5. Add a keyword, such as "Marketing," in the search bar.

Result: Google Drive narrows the results to presentations shared by Alex in the last week related to marketing.

Example 3: Searching for Images from a Team Event

If you need to find photos from your team's annual retreat:

1. In the search bar, click the **filter icon**.

2. Under **File type**, choose **Images**.

3. Enter a keyword, such as "Retreat," in the search bar.

4. If the event occurred a year ago, set the **Date modified** filter to the specific month and year.

5. (Optional) Add a location filter if you know the images were stored in a folder like "Team Events."

Result: Google Drive shows only image files related to the team retreat during the specified timeframe.

Example 4: Finding Shared Files from a Specific Folder

You want to locate a budget file stored in the "Finance 2024" folder:

1. Open the search bar and click on the **filter icon**.

2. Set the **Location** filter to the folder **Finance 2024**.

3. Type "Budget" in the search bar.

4. Optionally, set the **File type** filter to **Spreadsheets** if you're specifically looking for Google Sheets files.

Result: The search returns all spreadsheet files containing the word "Budget" within the "Finance 2024" folder.

Example 5: Using Boolean Operators for Complex Searches

You're looking for a file about "Training" but don't want drafts to appear in the results:

1. In the search bar, type:

2. Training NOT Draft

3. Use the **Date modified** filter to limit results to the last six months.

Result: Google Drive excludes all files with "Draft" in their name or content and displays only relevant training files.

These examples demonstrate the versatility and efficiency of Google Drive's search filters. By practicing and applying these methods, you'll become adept at locating files quickly, even in large and complex drives.

3.3.2 Recent Files

When working with Google Drive, the Recent Files feature serves as a quick and efficient way to access files you've worked on or interacted with recently. This tool is particularly helpful for those who manage multiple files and need to retrieve documents swiftly without sifting through an extensive folder hierarchy.

What are Recent Files?

The Recent Files section displays a chronological list of files you have opened, edited, or interacted with. This list updates automatically, making it a dynamic resource for quick access to your most current work. Files appear regardless of their type—documents, spreadsheets, presentations, PDFs, or images—all are included.

Recent Files is accessible in the main interface of Google Drive. When you log in, you'll typically see a section labeled **"Recent"** in the left-hand navigation panel. Clicking on it opens a streamlined view of all files you've worked on, organized by the last accessed date.

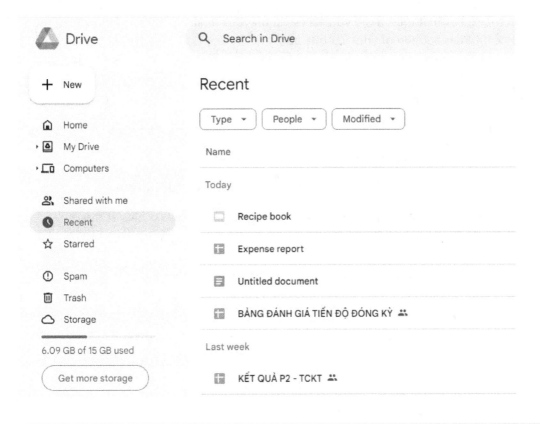

Why Use Recent Files?

There are several benefits to utilizing Recent Files:

1. **Time Efficiency:**

   Instead of navigating through folders to locate a document, you can quickly retrieve it from the Recent Files list. This saves significant time, particularly for users with complex file systems or a high volume of documents.

2. **Reduced Frustration:**

   Have you ever forgotten the exact name or location of a file? Recent Files eliminates the guesswork by placing your most-used files at your fingertips.

3. **Cross-Device Synchronization:**
   Recent Files isn't limited to a single device. Any activity performed on Google Drive—whether on a computer, tablet, or smartphone—syncs across all your

devices. For instance, a file you accessed on your desktop will also appear in the Recent Files section of your mobile app.

How to Access Recent Files

1. **Desktop Interface:**

   o   Open Google Drive in your browser.

   o   Locate the left-hand navigation panel and click on **"Recent."**

   o   Browse the displayed list, organized with the newest files at the top.

2. **Mobile App:**

   o   Open the Google Drive app on your device.

   o   Tap the **"Recent"** tab at the bottom of the screen.

   o   Scroll through the list of files, which appear in reverse chronological order.

Features of the Recent Files Section

1. **Previewing Files:**

   Hover over a file in the Recent Files list to see a quick preview or use the **"Open with"** feature for supported formats. Previews allow you to confirm that the file is the one you need without fully opening it.

2. **Sorting Options:**

   By default, files are sorted by the date and time of last access. However, you can use filters to refine the list further, such as limiting the display to specific file types like PDFs or presentations.

3. **File Actions:**

   From the Recent Files view, you can perform all standard file actions: open, share, rename, move to another folder, or delete. Simply right-click on the file (or use the menu icon on mobile) to access these options.

4. **Highlighting Starred Files:**

   Files marked with a star appear in the Recent Files list as well, but they also carry a star icon for easier identification. If you consistently use certain files, consider starring them for quicker recognition.

Best Practices for Managing Recent Files

1. **Review the List Regularly:**

   If you frequently access sensitive or confidential documents, take time to review your Recent Files list. This ensures you don't accidentally share or display files you didn't intend to expose.

2. **Combine Recent with Search Filters:**

   While the Recent Files list is handy, combining it with search filters (discussed in Section 3.3.1) can help you locate specific files even faster. For instance, if you're searching for a presentation you worked on last week, filter the Recent Files view by file type and date range.

3. **Pin Important Files:**

   While not directly tied to the Recent Files list, pinning essential files to your Google Drive homepage or adding them to starred folders ensures they remain easily accessible alongside recently used files.

Limitations of Recent Files

Despite its convenience, the Recent Files feature does have some limitations:

1. **File Deletion:**

   If a file has been deleted (either intentionally or accidentally), it won't appear in the Recent Files list. Always double-check the Trash if you suspect a file has been removed.

2. **Offline Access:**

The Recent Files section is only available when you're connected to the internet. To access files offline, make sure you've enabled offline mode and downloaded the necessary files beforehand.

3. **Shared Files Visibility:**

While files you've interacted with appear in the list, they may not include every file shared with you unless you've opened them at least once. For collaboration-heavy users, double-check the **Shared with Me** section for missing files.

Advanced Tips for Recent Files

1. **Keyboard Shortcuts:**
Use shortcuts to access Recent Files faster on the desktop. For example:

   o Press **Shift + R** to open the Recent Files tab directly.

2. **Integration with Google Workspace Apps:**

Recent Files isn't limited to Google Drive. You can access the same list directly within apps like Google Docs, Sheets, or Slides. Look for the **"Recent"** tab when opening a new file.

3. **Searching by Activity:**

If you collaborate on a file and someone else makes changes, it will also appear in the Recent Files list, keeping you updated on shared projects.

4. **Mobile-Friendly Tips:**

Add the Google Drive widget to your mobile device's home screen. This widget often includes direct access to recent files, saving you additional navigation steps.

Summary

The Recent Files feature in Google Drive is a powerful tool for streamlining your workflow and ensuring you have immediate access to your most-used documents. By mastering its use, you'll save time, reduce frustration, and improve your overall productivity.

Whether you're a student juggling multiple assignments, a professional managing projects, or simply someone looking to stay organized, leveraging the Recent Files section will undoubtedly enhance your Google Drive experience.

CHAPTER IV
Sharing and Collaborating

4.1 Sharing Files and Folders

4.1.1 Setting Permissions

Sharing files and folders is one of Google Drive's most powerful features, enabling users to collaborate seamlessly with others. Before sharing, understanding how to set permissions is essential to ensure the right level of access for your collaborators. In this section, we'll explore the types of permissions available, how to apply them effectively, and some best practices for secure collaboration.

What Are Permissions in Google Drive?

Permissions determine how others interact with the files or folders you share. Google Drive offers three primary permission levels:

1. **Viewer:** The recipient can view the file or folder but cannot make changes or leave comments.

2. **Commenter:** The recipient can add comments and suggestions but cannot directly edit the content.

3. **Editor:** The recipient has full access to edit the file or folder, including adding or deleting content.

Each permission level is designed to accommodate different collaboration needs. For example, sharing a file with a viewer is ideal when you want someone to review a document without making changes, while granting editor access is perfect for co-authors working together on a project.

How to Set Permissions in Google Drive

1. Sharing a File or Folder:
To share a file or folder, follow these steps:

1. Right-click the file or folder you want to share and select **"Share"** from the context menu.

2. In the sharing dialog box, enter the email addresses of the people you want to share with.

3. Select the permission level for each person (Viewer, Commenter, or Editor).

4. Click **"Send"** to share the file or folder.

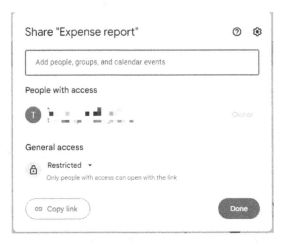

2. Customizing Permissions for Groups:
If you're sharing with multiple people, you can assign different permissions to each recipient. For instance, you can give editing rights to your core team while limiting others to viewing only.

3. Adjusting Permissions After Sharing:
You can modify permissions at any time. To do this:

*   Open the sharing settings for the file or folder.

*   Locate the person or group whose permissions you want to adjust.

*   Change their access level or remove their access altogether.

Using Advanced Sharing Options

Google Drive also provides advanced sharing features to enhance control over your files:

1. Expiring Access:
For sensitive documents, you can set expiration dates for access. This is especially useful when sharing files with external collaborators for a limited time.

2. Preventing Download or Copying:
When sharing as a Viewer or Commenter, you can disable options for downloading, printing, or copying the file. This adds an extra layer of security.

3. Sharing with a Link:

Instead of specifying individual email addresses, you can create a shareable link. The link can be restricted to your organization, accessible to anyone with the link, or limited to invited users. Always double-check the link permissions to avoid accidental over-sharing.

Best Practices for Setting Permissions

To make the most of Google Drive's sharing capabilities while maintaining security, follow these best practices:

1. **Start with the Least Privilege Principle:**

   Only grant the permissions necessary for the task. If someone only needs to view a document, avoid giving them editing rights.

2. **Review Permissions Regularly:**

   Periodically audit shared files and folders to ensure permissions are still appropriate. Remove access for individuals who no longer need it.

3. **Use Shared Drives for Teams:**

   For team projects, consider using a **Shared Drive**. This ensures files are owned collectively by the team rather than an individual, simplifying permission management.

4. **Be Mindful of External Sharing:**

When sharing outside your organization, double-check the recipient's email address and set expiration dates or restrict actions where necessary.

5. **Communicate with Collaborators:**

   Let recipients know their level of access and what is expected of them. For example, if you share a document for feedback, clarify whether they should use comments or suggestions.

Common Scenarios and Solutions

Scenario 1: *Sharing a Report with a Team*

You've created a monthly performance report and want your team to review it. Set permissions as follows:

- **Managers:** Editor (to update specific sections).

- **Team Members:** Commenter (to provide feedback).

- **External Stakeholders:** Viewer (to review the final report).

Scenario 2: *Collaborating on a Marketing Plan*

Your marketing team is drafting a plan with external consultants. Use a shareable link with editing rights, but enable expiration dates and disable downloading to maintain control over sensitive data.

Scenario 3: *Managing Permissions for a Large Project*

For a cross-departmental project with dozens of files, create a shared folder. Assign viewer access to general team members and editor access to project leads.

Troubleshooting Permission Issues

1. **Recipient Cannot Access the File:**

   o   Double-check their email address.

   o   Ensure you've selected the correct permission level.

     o Confirm the recipient has signed in with the same email address you shared the file with.

2. **Unauthorized Changes to a File:**

     o Check the file's version history to identify the changes.

     o Adjust permissions to limit editing rights.

3. **Accidental Over-Sharing:**

     o Review and restrict link-sharing settings.

     o Use the activity dashboard to track file access.

Mastering permission settings in Google Drive not only improves collaboration but also ensures the security and integrity of your files. Whether you're sharing a personal photo album or collaborating on a business proposal, these tools and tips will help you manage access effectively. In the next section, we'll dive deeper into **Sharing Links** and how they can simplify collaboration even further.

4.1.2 Sharing Links

Sharing files and folders in Google Drive via links is one of the simplest and most effective ways to collaborate with others. This method allows you to create a link to your file or folder and share it directly with individuals or groups, making it accessible to the right audience without requiring additional permissions. Here's a comprehensive guide to understanding and using the "Share via Link" feature effectively.

What is a Sharing Link?

A sharing link is a unique URL generated by Google Drive that connects directly to your file or folder. Once created, this link can be shared with others, giving them access to your content based on the permission settings you choose.

For instance:

- **View only**: Others can see the file but cannot make changes.

- **Comment**: Others can add comments and suggestions but cannot edit the main content.

- **Edit**: Full access to modify the file, make changes, or even delete it.

How to Share Files or Folders Using Links

1. **Select the File or Folder**
   Open Google Drive and locate the file or folder you want to share. Right-click on it, then choose "Get Link" from the menu.

2. **Set Permissions**
   By default, Google Drive sets the link to "Restricted," meaning only people added explicitly can access it. To broaden access:

   o   Click the dropdown menu under "Restricted."

   o   Change it to "Anyone with the link."

3. **Choose the Role**
   Decide what others can do with the file:

   o   **Viewer**: They can only see the file.

   o   **Commenter**: They can leave feedback without altering the content.

   o   **Editor**: They can fully modify the file.

4. **Copy and Share the Link**
   After setting the appropriate permissions, click "Copy Link." Paste this link into an email, messaging app, or other communication platform to share it.

When to Use Sharing Links

Using sharing links is ideal in several scenarios:

- **Quick Sharing with Large Groups**: Instead of adding each person's email individually, a single link can give access to everyone who needs it.

- **Posting in Public Spaces**: For content intended for broader audiences, such as a shared company policy or a public presentation.

- **Simplifying Collaboration**: Sharing a link ensures collaborators can quickly access the file without waiting for manual permissions.

Best Practices for Sharing Links

1. **Set Clear Permissions**
   Always ensure you're granting only the necessary level of access. For example:

   - Use "Viewer" mode for read-only documents.

   - Use "Editor" mode only with trusted collaborators.

2. **Use Descriptive File Names**
   A well-labeled file name helps recipients quickly identify the purpose of the file or folder.

3. **Include a Clear Context**
   When sharing a link, add a message explaining its purpose and any actions you expect from the recipients. For example:

   - *"Here's the draft of the marketing plan. Please leave comments by Friday."*

4. **Set Expiration Dates**
   For sensitive documents, set an expiration date for the link. This ensures the file is only accessible for a limited time.

Enhancing Security When Sharing Links

1. **Password Protection**
   While Google Drive itself doesn't offer password protection, third-party tools can add this layer of security if needed.

2. **Avoid Sharing with "Anyone with the Link"**
   For confidential files, limit access to specific individuals instead of enabling access for anyone with the link.

3. **Regularly Audit Shared Links**
   Over time, you might forget who has access to your files. Periodically review your sharing settings to revoke unnecessary permissions.

4. **Monitor Activity**
   Use Google Drive's "Activity" pane to track who has viewed or edited the file.

Common Challenges and Solutions

1. **Recipients Can't Access the File**
   If someone reports issues accessing the file, double-check the link's permissions. Ensure it's not set to "Restricted."

2. **Accidental Sharing of Confidential Information**
   If you mistakenly share sensitive data, immediately change the file's permissions or revoke the link.

3. **Unwanted Edits or Comments**
   If collaborators make unwanted changes, use the "Version History" feature to restore an earlier version of the file.

Creative Ways to Use Sharing Links

1. **Team Collaboration**

   Create a shared folder for a project and generate a link to distribute to all team members. This ensures everyone has centralized access to all relevant documents.

2. **Educational Purposes**
   Teachers can share lecture notes, assignments, or reading materials with students via links.

3. **Business Use**
   Use links to share proposals, reports, or presentations with clients or stakeholders.

4. **Publications and Portfolios**
   Share your work portfolio or research papers using view-only links for potential employers or collaborators.

Troubleshooting Issues with Sharing Links

1. **Broken Links**

   If recipients report a broken link, check whether the file or folder was moved or renamed. Such changes can invalidate the link.

2. **Overwhelmed by Permissions Management**

   Consider using shared drives for larger teams to streamline permissions management.

3. **Link Clutter in Communication Channels**

   Use tools like link shorteners (e.g., bit.ly) to create cleaner, more manageable URLs.

Sharing links in Google Drive is a powerful feature that simplifies collaboration while ensuring flexibility and control over access. By mastering the art of link sharing, you'll be able to work efficiently, securely, and effectively with teams, clients, and partners.

4.2 Real-Time Collaboration

4.2.1 Adding Comments

Collaboration lies at the heart of Google Drive's functionality, and commenting is one of the most effective tools for fostering communication. The commenting feature in Google Drive allows users to share feedback, provide clarification, or suggest changes directly within a file. This makes Google Drive ideal for group projects, team workflows, and any situation that requires ongoing discussion and input.

In this section, we will explore the commenting feature in detail, including its purpose, how to use it, and best practices for effective collaboration.

Understanding the Purpose of Comments

Comments are annotations that provide context or instructions related to specific parts of a file. Unlike editing, comments are non-intrusive—they do not alter the actual content of a document, spreadsheet, or presentation. This feature is especially useful for:

- **Providing Feedback**: Team members can point out areas for improvement or share insights without making permanent changes.

- **Clarifying Content**: Comments can clarify complex ideas, helping all collaborators stay on the same page.

- **Tracking Suggestions**: Comments create a trail of suggestions and discussions, ensuring transparency and accountability.

How to Add Comments in Google Drive Files

Step 1: Select the Text, Cell, or Slide

To add a comment, you first need to highlight the specific area of the file you want to comment on. For example:

- In Google Docs, highlight a word, phrase, or paragraph.

- In Google Sheets, click on the relevant cell or range of cells.

- In Google Slides, click on the object, text box, or image you want to reference.

Step 2: Open the Comment Tool

There are multiple ways to open the comment tool:

- **Right-Click Method**: Right-click on the selected text or object and choose "Comment" from the context menu.

- **Toolbar Method**: Click the speech bubble icon on the toolbar, usually located at the top right corner of the file interface.

- **Keyboard Shortcut**: Use Ctrl + Alt + M (Windows) or Cmd + Option + M (Mac) to open the comment tool instantly.

Step 3: Enter Your Comment

Type your feedback or message into the comment box. If the comment is directed to a specific person, you can tag them by typing @ followed by their email address or name. This action sends a notification to the tagged individual, drawing their attention to the comment.

Step 4: Post the Comment

Click the "Comment" button to post your input. Once added, the comment will appear as a small speech bubble icon in the margin (for Docs and Slides) or as a flag in the corner of the cell (for Sheets).

Responding to Comments

Collaboration often involves discussions, and Google Drive's commenting system facilitates this with threaded replies. When someone posts a comment, others can respond directly below it. Here's how:

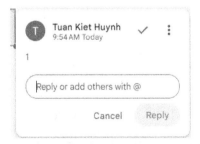

- **Click on the Comment Icon**: Navigate to the relevant comment by clicking on its icon in the document or spreadsheet.

- **Type Your Reply**: Use the text box below the original comment to add your response.

- **Resolve or Keep the Thread Open**: If the issue has been addressed, click the "Resolve" button to close the thread. However, unresolved comments remain visible for ongoing discussion.

Tagging Collaborators in Comments

Tagging is a powerful way to ensure that specific individuals are notified about comments. To tag someone:

- Type @ or + followed by the person's email address or name.

- Google Drive will display a list of matching contacts. Select the correct individual.

- Once tagged, the person will receive an email notification with a link to the file and comment.

This feature is particularly helpful for assigning tasks, as it allows collaborators to know exactly what action is needed from them.

Editing or Deleting Comments

Occasionally, you might need to edit or remove a comment. Here's how:

- **To Edit**: Click on the three-dot menu (⋮) next to the comment and select "Edit." Update the text as needed.

- **To Delete**: Use the same menu to select "Delete," permanently removing the comment. Note that deleted comments cannot be recovered, so ensure you no longer need them before proceeding.

Best Practices for Adding Comments

To make the most out of the commenting feature, consider the following best practices:

1. **Be Specific**: Avoid vague feedback. Clearly indicate the issue or provide actionable suggestions.

- o   Instead of: "This part is unclear."

- o   Try: "Could you elaborate on how this data supports the conclusion?"

2. **Keep It Professional**: Remember that comments are visible to all collaborators. Maintain a respectful and constructive tone.

3. **Use Tags Effectively**: Only tag individuals who are directly involved in the discussion to avoid overwhelming others with unnecessary notifications.

4. **Resolve Comments Promptly**: Once an issue has been addressed, resolve the comment to keep the file organized.

5. **Document Decisions**: Use comments to record important decisions or agreements made during the collaboration process.

Use Cases for Adding Comments

1. **Group Projects**: Students working on a joint assignment can use comments to divide tasks, provide feedback, and clarify details.

2. **Team Workflows**: Teams can discuss revisions or updates directly within the file, eliminating the need for back-and-forth emails.

3. **Client Feedback**: Clients reviewing a draft can leave comments instead of making direct edits, preserving the original content.

Conclusion

Adding comments in Google Drive files is a simple yet powerful way to enhance collaboration. By allowing users to provide feedback, ask questions, and track suggestions, the commenting feature fosters transparency and teamwork. Whether you're working on a group project or refining a document for publication, mastering this tool will make your collaborative efforts more efficient and productive.

4.2.2 Suggesting Edits

Collaboration in Google Drive becomes even more effective with the *Suggesting Mode* feature, particularly in Google Docs. This mode allows team members to propose edits without directly altering the original text. Instead, the changes are displayed as suggestions that can be reviewed and accepted or rejected by the document owner or collaborators with appropriate permissions.

What is Suggesting Mode?

Suggesting Mode is one of three editing modes available in Google Docs:

- **Editing Mode**: Directly modifies the document.

- **Viewing Mode**: Allows users to view the document without making changes.

- **Suggesting Mode**: Allows users to propose changes, which appear as tracked edits for others to review.

By default, documents open in Editing Mode, but users can switch to Suggesting Mode to contribute in a more controlled and non-intrusive way. This is particularly useful in collaborative environments where clarity and accountability are important.

How to Enable Suggesting Mode

To activate Suggesting Mode:

1. Open a Google Doc you wish to edit.

2. In the top-right corner of the toolbar, locate the pencil icon or the current mode indicator.

3. Click it and select **Suggesting** from the dropdown menu.

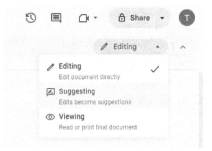

Once in Suggesting Mode, any text added appears in a different color, and deletions are shown as strike-throughs. Each suggestion is accompanied by a comment box where collaborators can discuss the changes.

Benefits of Suggesting Mode

1. **Enhanced Collaboration**: It ensures that team members can contribute without overriding each other's work.

2. **Clear Accountability**: Each suggestion is tagged with the editor's name, making it easy to track contributions.

3. **Simplified Decision-Making**: Document owners can review suggestions systematically, deciding which to implement.

4. **Preserving the Original**: The original text remains intact until a suggestion is accepted, preventing unintended errors.

Practical Scenarios for Suggesting Mode

1. **Team Projects**: Members can propose rephrasing or restructuring ideas without disrupting the flow.

2. **Proofreading and Editing**: Editors can highlight grammatical errors or awkward phrasings for the writer to review.

3. **Policy and Procedure Updates**: Suggesting Mode is ideal for refining official documents collaboratively while ensuring proper oversight.

Making Suggestions

When making suggestions, follow these best practices:

1. **Be Specific**: Provide clear and actionable recommendations. Instead of saying "Make this clearer," propose alternative wording.

2. **Use Comments Strategically**: When your suggestion needs further explanation, add a comment to clarify your rationale.

3. **Respect Tone and Style**: Align your suggestions with the document's intended voice and purpose.

4. **Avoid Overloading**: Suggest only meaningful changes to keep the review process manageable.

For example, if a sentence reads:
"The project was delayed due to unforeseen circumstances,"

you could suggest changing it to:

"The project experienced a delay because of unexpected challenges."

Responding to Suggestions

As a document owner or collaborator with editing rights, responding to suggestions is straightforward:

1. Hover over the suggestion in the document.

2. Use the checkmark to accept the change, which automatically incorporates it into the text.

3. Use the "X" to reject the suggestion, which removes it while keeping the original text intact.

Each action is logged in the document's *Version History*, preserving a clear record of changes.

Managing Feedback in Suggesting Mode

When multiple collaborators are suggesting edits, maintaining order is crucial:

1. **Assign Roles**: Designate specific collaborators to review suggestions to streamline decision-making.

2. **Group Similar Suggestions**: Address related changes together for efficiency.

3. **Resolve Disputes Through Comments**: Use the commenting feature to discuss disagreements before deciding.

Advanced Tips for Suggesting Mode

1. **Tagging Collaborators**: Use "@" followed by a person's name to notify them directly of your comment or suggestion.

2. **Integrating Suggesting Mode with Comments**: Link suggestions to relevant comments for a comprehensive discussion.

3. **Using Keyboard Shortcuts**: Learn shortcuts for suggesting mode (e.g., Ctrl + / on Windows or Cmd + / on Mac to open menus faster).

4. **Reviewing All Suggestions at Once**: Use the "Review Suggested Edits" option to accept or reject multiple suggestions in bulk.

Challenges and How to Overcome Them

1. **Overlapping Suggestions**: Multiple collaborators may suggest similar changes, leading to clutter. Regularly consolidate and review suggestions to avoid redundancy.

2. **Misinterpretation of Suggestions**: Ambiguity in suggestions can slow down the process. Adding comments and using precise language helps mitigate this.

3. **Excessive Suggestions**: A high volume of edits can overwhelm the document owner. Set clear guidelines on what types of changes should be suggested.

Suggesting Mode in Other Google Apps

While Suggesting Mode is primarily associated with Google Docs, similar features exist in other Google Workspace apps:

- **Google Sheets**: Use the *Comment* feature to propose changes to data or formulas.

- **Google Slides**: Suggest edits through comments on specific slides or elements.

- **Google Drive**: Annotate PDF files or images with suggestions and notes.

Wrapping Up

Suggesting Mode in Google Docs empowers teams to collaborate effectively while maintaining control over document integrity. By leveraging this feature, teams can streamline workflows, ensure accountability, and create polished, well-reviewed documents. As you grow accustomed to this mode, you'll find it indispensable for projects requiring multiple contributors and meticulous attention to detail.

4.3 Managing Shared Drives

Shared Drives in Google Drive are powerful tools for collaboration, particularly for teams and organizations that need to work on shared files and folders seamlessly. Unlike personal Google Drive folders, Shared Drives provide a structured environment where files are owned collectively by the team rather than an individual. This distinction brings unique advantages and management considerations. In this section, we'll explore everything you need to know about managing Shared Drives effectively.

What are Shared Drives?

A Shared Drive is a collaborative space within Google Drive where multiple users can store, access, and manage files. Unlike individual Google Drives, where files are owned by the person who uploads them, files in a Shared Drive are owned by the team. This means that even if a team member leaves the organization, the files remain accessible to the rest of the team.

Key Features of Shared Drives:

- **Centralized Ownership:** Files are owned by the team, not individuals.

- **Flexible Permissions:** Administrators can control who can view, comment, edit, or manage files.

- **Improved Collaboration:** Shared Drives streamline teamwork by organizing files in a single, accessible location.

Creating and Setting Up a Shared Drive

Creating a Shared Drive is straightforward. However, to ensure its long-term usability, it's essential to plan its structure and permissions carefully.

Steps to Create a Shared Drive:

1. **Access Google Drive:** Log in to your Google Workspace account and navigate to the "Shared Drives" section in the sidebar.

2. **Click "+ New":** Select "New Shared Drive" to create a new drive.

3. **Name Your Drive:** Choose a name that reflects the drive's purpose, such as "Marketing Team Files" or "Project Alpha."

Best Practices for Setting Up a Shared Drive:

- **Define a Clear Purpose:** Establish the drive's purpose to avoid confusion among users.

- **Organize by Categories:** Create folders based on project phases, departments, or document types.

- **Assign Roles and Permissions:** Limit editing rights to key contributors while allowing broader access for viewing or commenting.

Managing Permissions in Shared Drives

Permissions in Shared Drives are more nuanced than in individual drives. Managers can assign specific roles to team members to control their level of access.

Roles in Shared Drives:

1. **Manager:** Full access to manage members, permissions, and content.

2. **Contributor:** Can add and edit files but cannot delete them.

3. **Content Manager:** Can organize and edit content within the drive.

4. **Viewer:** Can view files but cannot make changes.

5. **Commenter:** Can add comments without editing content.

How to Manage Permissions:

1. Open the Shared Drive.

2. Click on "Manage Members" or "Share."

3. Add new members or groups by entering their email addresses.

4. Select the appropriate role for each person.

Structuring and Organizing Files

A well-organized Shared Drive is crucial for efficient collaboration. Without proper structure, files can become difficult to locate and manage.

Tips for Organizing Files:

- **Use Descriptive Folder Names:** Ensure that folder names are intuitive, such as "2024 Budget Reports" or "Client Proposals."

- **Adopt Naming Conventions:** Standardize file names to include dates, project names, or version numbers (e.g., "Project_Plan_v2.docx").

- **Regular Maintenance:** Periodically review and archive outdated files to keep the drive clutter-free.

Using Shared Drives for Team Projects

Shared Drives are ideal for managing team projects that require collaboration across departments or locations.

Steps for Using Shared Drives in Projects:

1. **Create a Project-Specific Drive:** Set up a dedicated Shared Drive for the project.

2. **Assign Roles:** Define roles and responsibilities for each team member.

3. **Integrate Tools:** Use Google Docs, Sheets, and Slides for real-time collaboration.

4. **Track Progress:** Use file comments and version history to monitor changes.

Troubleshooting Common Issues

Despite their benefits, Shared Drives can occasionally present challenges.

Common Issues and Solutions:

- **Issue:** Files are missing from the drive.
    - **Solution:** Check the drive's activity log to identify recent changes.

- **Issue:** Users cannot access files.
    - **Solution:** Verify that permissions are correctly assigned.

- **Issue:** Drive space is running low.

    o **Solution:** Delete unnecessary files or upgrade storage plans.

Security and Compliance in Shared Drives

Maintaining security is critical, especially when Shared Drives contain sensitive information.

Security Tips:

- **Enable Two-Factor Authentication:** Protect accounts with an additional layer of security.

- **Regularly Audit Access:** Review and update permissions to ensure only authorized users have access.

- **Use DLP Rules:** If using Google Workspace, enable Data Loss Prevention (DLP) policies to prevent sensitive data from being shared externally.

Benefits of Shared Drives

Using Shared Drives provides several advantages for teams:

- **Improved Collaboration:** Centralized storage enhances teamwork and reduces duplication of effort.

- **Scalability:** Shared Drives grow with your team, accommodating new members and projects.

- **Reliability:** Files remain accessible even if contributors leave the team.

By mastering Shared Drives, you can significantly improve your team's productivity and organization. Whether you're working on a small project or managing a large team, Shared Drives provide the tools and flexibility to keep everyone on the same page.

CHAPTER V
Advanced Features

5.1 Using Google Drive Offline

In a world where internet connectivity is almost ubiquitous, there are still times when you may find yourself needing access to your files without a reliable connection. Whether you're traveling, working in remote locations, or experiencing network outages, Google Drive offers a robust offline mode that allows you to view and edit your files without an active internet connection. This section covers the essentials of setting up and using Google Drive offline, ensuring you're never caught unprepared.

5.1.1 Setting Up Offline Access

To work offline with Google Drive, you need to enable specific settings and meet a few requirements. Here's a detailed, step-by-step guide to setting up offline access.

Understanding Offline Mode

Google Drive's offline mode allows users to access Google Docs, Sheets, and Slides even when disconnected from the internet. Changes made offline are saved locally and synced to the cloud as soon as the connection is restored. This feature ensures uninterrupted productivity, no matter where you are.

Requirements for Offline Access

Before setting up offline access, you need to confirm a few prerequisites:

- **Browser:** Offline mode works best with Google Chrome. While other browsers may support limited offline features, Chrome offers the most seamless experience.

- **Google Account:** Ensure you're signed in to your Google account. Offline settings are specific to each account and device.

- **Storage Space:** Make sure your device has enough storage space to download files locally for offline use.

- **Internet Connection (Initially):** Offline mode must be enabled while you're connected to the internet.

Step-by-Step Guide to Enable Offline Mode

1. Install Google Chrome (if needed)

If you haven't already, download and install Google Chrome. This browser is optimized for Google Drive offline features.

2. Open Google Drive in Chrome

Navigate to Google Drive and log in to your account.

3. Enable Offline Mode

- Click on the gear icon (⚙) in the upper-right corner to open the settings menu.

- Select **Settings** from the dropdown menu.

- In the settings window, locate the **Offline** section.

- Check the box that says **"Create, open, and edit your recent Google Docs, Sheets, and Slides files on this device while offline."**

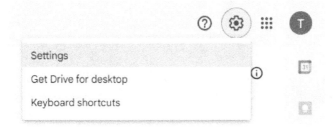

Offline

☐   Create, open and edit your recent Google Docs, Sheets, and Slides files on this device while offline

     Not recommended on public or shared computers. Learn more

4. Install the Google Docs Offline Extension

For a more seamless offline experience, install the **Google Docs Offline** extension from the Chrome Web Store.

- Go to the Google Docs Offline extension.

- Click **Add to Chrome** and follow the prompts to complete the installation.

5. Select Files for Offline Access

By default, Google Drive will make your most recent files available offline. However, you can manually choose specific files or folders:

- Right-click on a file or folder in Google Drive.

- Select **Available offline** from the menu.
  A small checkmark icon will appear next to the file, indicating it is ready for offline use.

6. Test Offline Access

Once offline mode is enabled, test it by disconnecting from the internet:

- Turn off your Wi-Fi or unplug your Ethernet cable.

- Open Google Chrome and navigate to Google Drive.

- Confirm that your files and folders are accessible. You should be able to view and edit them as usual.

Managing Offline Files

Managing which files are available offline is essential to optimize your device's storage space:

- **View Offline Files:** To see all files available offline, go to the Google Drive app and filter by "Offline" from the left sidebar.

- **Remove Offline Access:** If you no longer need certain files offline, right-click on them and deselect **Available offline** to free up storage space.

Tips for an Optimized Offline Experience

- **Plan Ahead:** If you know you'll be offline, pre-select files or folders you'll need to avoid last-minute delays.

- **Keep Your Chrome Browser Updated:** Ensure you're using the latest version of Chrome for the best offline performance.

- **Regularly Sync Changes:** Reconnect to the internet periodically to ensure your changes are uploaded and to download updates made by collaborators.

- **Work with Recent Files:** Offline mode prioritizes files you've accessed recently, so make sure to open important documents ahead of time.

Troubleshooting Offline Mode

While offline mode is generally reliable, you may encounter occasional issues. Here's how to resolve them:

- **Offline Option Not Available:** Check that the Google Docs Offline extension is installed and your browser is updated.

- **Files Not Syncing:** Reconnect to the internet and wait a few minutes for changes to sync.

- **Storage Issues:** If your device runs out of storage, reduce the number of files marked for offline access.

Why Offline Mode Matters

Enabling offline access not only ensures you remain productive during outages but also provides peace of mind when working with critical documents. Whether you're on a plane, in a rural area, or simply dealing with temporary network disruptions, offline mode keeps your work flowing seamlessly.

In the next section, we'll explore how to synchronize changes made offline with your online Google Drive account.

5.1.2 Syncing Changes

Using Google Drive offline can be a game-changer when you're working in areas with limited or no internet connectivity. However, ensuring that your changes are properly synced once you reconnect to the internet is critical for maintaining data consistency and avoiding conflicts. In this section, we'll explore the process of syncing changes effectively, tips for troubleshooting sync issues, and best practices for offline workflows.

Understanding How Syncing Works

When you work offline in Google Drive, any changes you make to files—whether it's creating new content, editing existing documents, or reorganizing folders—are saved locally on your device. Google Drive's offline mode uses your browser's storage or your device's memory to temporarily hold these changes. Once you're back online, Google Drive automatically detects the network connection and syncs these offline changes with the cloud.

Syncing works in both directions:

- **Uploading Changes:** Offline edits and new files created are uploaded to the cloud.

- **Downloading Updates:** Changes made by collaborators while you were offline are updated on your device.

This two-way synchronization ensures that everyone working on shared files has access to the most recent versions.

Steps for Syncing Offline Changes

1. **Reconnect to the Internet:**

- o Open your browser or Google Drive app once you're back online. Google Drive will automatically begin syncing. You'll see a small status icon next to your files, indicating the sync process.

2. **Monitor Sync Status:**

- o In your browser, you'll notice a circular arrow icon on the Google Drive tab, showing that syncing is in progress. On the desktop app, the sync status can be checked in the system tray (Windows) or the menu bar (Mac).

3. **Resolve Conflicts:**

- o If there are conflicts between changes made offline and updates from other collaborators, Google Drive will prompt you to choose which version to keep or merge changes where possible.

4. **Verify Completion:**

- o Open your Google Drive account in your browser or app and check the "Recent" section to confirm that all offline changes have been uploaded.

Common Issues and Fixes in Syncing

1. **Changes Not Syncing Automatically:**

- o Ensure that you're logged into the same Google account you used while working offline.

- o Check your internet connection stability. Even minor disruptions can pause the sync process.

- o Restart your browser or Google Drive app to refresh the sync status.

2. **Conflicting Edits:**

- o Google Drive flags conflicts by creating duplicate versions of files, labeled with the conflicting user's name. To resolve this, compare the versions and merge the changes manually.

3. **Offline Mode Not Activating Properly:**

o Double-check that offline mode is enabled for your account. Open Google Drive in your browser, navigate to settings, and ensure the "Offline" checkbox is selected.

4. **Sync Process Freezing:**

o Freezing is often caused by low storage space. Clear unused files from your device or cloud to free up resources.

Best Practices for Seamless Offline Syncing

1. **Save Regularly While Working Offline:**

o Although Google Drive auto-saves frequently, it's good practice to manually save before closing your browser or app to ensure your edits are recorded.

2. **Organize Files Before Disconnecting:**

o Set up a clear folder structure and download all necessary files in advance. This reduces the risk of missing critical documents when offline.

3. **Limit Offline Edits on Shared Files:**

o If multiple people are working on the same file, offline changes can lead to version conflicts. To avoid this, communicate with collaborators and minimize concurrent offline editing.

4. **Check Sync Logs After Reconnecting:**

o Google Drive provides a brief activity log showing which files were synced. Review this log to ensure that no changes were missed.

Advanced Tips for Efficient Offline Syncing

1. **Using Google Drive Desktop App:**

The desktop app (Google Drive for Desktop) offers a more robust offline experience compared to the browser. It automatically syncs entire folders to your device and provides real-time updates once online.

2. **Sync Priority Settings:**
   In the desktop app, you can prioritize certain files or folders to sync first. Use this feature for time-sensitive documents.

3. **Syncing Large Files:**

   Large files or videos may take longer to upload after reconnecting. Compress these files when possible, or prioritize syncing them separately to avoid delays in other uploads.

4. **Collaborator Notifications:**

   Inform collaborators about significant changes made offline. This ensures that everyone stays aligned and reduces the chances of duplicate work.

Troubleshooting Unresolved Sync Issues

If your offline changes still fail to sync, follow these steps:

- **Clear Browser Cache:** A cluttered cache can interfere with syncing in browser-based Google Drive.

- **Reauthorize Offline Mode:** Disable offline mode, refresh Google Drive, and enable offline mode again.

- **Reinstall Google Drive App:** For persistent issues in the desktop app, uninstall and reinstall the software. This resets the sync engine.

If these steps don't resolve the problem, contact Google Support for further assistance.

Conclusion

Syncing changes after working offline is a critical step to ensure your files remain accurate and up-to-date. By understanding the syncing process, following best practices, and proactively addressing issues, you can seamlessly transition between offline and online work environments. This not only saves time but also enhances collaboration and productivity when using Google Drive.

5.2 Integrating with Other Google Tools

5.2.1 Embedding Google Docs and Sheets

Integrating Google Docs and Sheets with Google Drive can significantly boost your productivity, making it easier to store, share, and manage essential documents in one seamless ecosystem. This section will explore how you can embed Google Docs and Sheets into your Drive, access them directly, and utilize their collaborative features.

What Does Embedding Mean in Google Drive?

In the context of Google Drive, "embedding" refers to integrating Google Docs and Sheets files in a way that allows for immediate access, real-time updates, and streamlined sharing. Unlike traditional storage, where files are static and need to be downloaded or uploaded repeatedly, embedding Google Docs and Sheets ensures that these files are always up-to-date and accessible from any device with internet access.

Benefits of Embedding Google Docs and Sheets

1. **Real-Time Collaboration**:
   - Embedded files in Google Drive can be edited in real time by multiple users. Whether working with a team or collaborating with clients, this feature eliminates the need for multiple file versions.
   - Changes made to the file are instantly saved and synchronized, ensuring everyone works on the most current version.

2. **Improved Organization**:
   - Embedding allows you to organize your Docs and Sheets within relevant folders. This reduces the chaos of searching for specific documents amidst a cluttered Drive.
   - By using appropriate naming conventions and folder hierarchies, your workflow becomes much more efficient.

3. **Access Anytime, Anywhere**:

   o   Embedded files are stored securely in the cloud, making them accessible across devices. Whether on a computer, tablet, or mobile phone, you can access and edit these documents seamlessly.

4. **Streamlined Sharing**:

   o   Sharing embedded Docs or Sheets is straightforward. You can adjust permissions for viewing, commenting, or editing within seconds.

How to Embed Google Docs in Google Drive

Step 1: Creating a Google Doc

1. Open Google Drive.

2. Click on the **New** button in the top-left corner.

3. Select **Google Docs** from the dropdown menu.

   o   This action creates a new blank document directly within your Drive.

4. Name your document by clicking the title field in the top-left corner of the page.

Step 2: Moving the Doc to the Right Folder

1. Click on the folder icon next to the file name.

2. Choose the folder where you want the file to reside. If the folder doesn't exist, click **New Folder** to create one.

3. Click **Move Here** to confirm.

Step 3: Accessing the Embedded Doc

- Once the Doc is stored in the desired folder, it remains accessible directly from Google Drive.

- You can preview, share, or edit it without downloading or transferring the file elsewhere.

How to Embed Google Sheets in Google Drive

Step 1: Creating a Google Sheet

1. Navigate to Google Drive.

2. Click on the **New** button, and select **Google Sheets** from the dropdown.

3. A blank spreadsheet opens, ready for data input.

4. Rename your file as described earlier for Google Docs.

Step 2: Structuring the Spreadsheet

- Google Sheets offers templates for a wide range of use cases, such as budgets, calendars, and project tracking.

- Use these templates to quickly set up a functional spreadsheet tailored to your needs.

Step 3: Organizing in Google Drive

- Similar to Docs, move the Sheet into the appropriate folder by using the folder icon next to the file name.

Collaboration Features of Embedded Docs and Sheets

1. **Commenting and Suggestions**:

   o Embedded files allow collaborators to leave comments or make suggestions.

   o Highlight specific text or cells, and right-click to add a comment. This is particularly useful for feedback and collaborative brainstorming.

2. **Version Control**:

   o Google Docs and Sheets keep track of every change made, ensuring that previous versions are always accessible.

   o By embedding these files in Google Drive, version history remains linked to the file, even when moved between folders.

3. **Notifications and Updates**:

- o Collaborators are notified of changes via email or within the Drive interface.

- o Embedded files ensure that changes are instantly reflected for all users.

Pro Tips for Embedding Google Docs and Sheets

1. **Use Descriptive File Names**:

   - o Naming files clearly helps you and your collaborators locate them quickly. For example, "Marketing_Plan_Q1_2024" is much more descriptive than "Document1".

2. **Leverage Folder Permissions**:

   - o Apply folder-wide permissions to streamline sharing for embedded files. This eliminates the need to set permissions for each individual file.

3. **Integrate with Google Calendar**:

   - o Link embedded Docs or Sheets to your Google Calendar events for easy access during meetings or project reviews.

4. **Utilize Keyboard Shortcuts**:

   - o Learn essential Google Docs and Sheets shortcuts to navigate and edit your files more efficiently.

Troubleshooting Common Issues

1. **Lost Access to Embedded Files**:

   - o If you lose access to an embedded file, check the sharing permissions. Ensure the owner has granted you the necessary access.

2. **File Not Syncing Properly**:

   - o This might occur due to temporary connectivity issues. Refresh the file or clear your browser cache to resolve the problem.

3. **Accidental Deletion of Embedded Files**:

○ Deleted files in Google Drive move to the Trash. You can recover them within 30 days by navigating to the Trash folder.

Case Study: Maximizing Team Collaboration

Imagine a marketing team working on a quarterly report. The lead creates a Google Doc for the report's narrative and a Google Sheet for data analysis. Both files are embedded in a shared Google Drive folder.

- Team members simultaneously update the Sheets with sales figures while the lead writes the report narrative in Docs.

- Comments and suggestions are used to refine the content collaboratively.

- When the report is finalized, the embedded files are shared with stakeholders, streamlining the entire review process.

This example demonstrates the power of embedding Google Docs and Sheets in Google Drive, enabling teams to work more efficiently and cohesively.

5.2.2 Linking with Google Calendar

Google Calendar is an essential productivity tool that seamlessly integrates with Google Drive to help you stay organized, schedule tasks effectively, and collaborate more efficiently. This section explores the powerful integration between Google Drive and Google Calendar, highlighting its practical applications, step-by-step instructions, and best practices for leveraging this integration in both personal and professional settings.

Understanding the Integration

At its core, Google Calendar and Google Drive work together to ensure your files and events are interconnected. Whether attaching documents to calendar events, setting up meeting agendas, or sharing resources, this integration bridges the gap between your schedules and your files.

The benefits include:

- **Centralized Information**: Keep all relevant documents tied to specific events, so you never have to hunt for files.

- **Streamlined Collaboration**: Share event-related materials with attendees, ensuring everyone is on the same page.

- **Time-Saving Features**: Quickly create or access Google Drive files directly from your calendar.

Linking Google Drive Files to Calendar Events

One of the most practical ways to use Google Drive with Google Calendar is by attaching files to events. This ensures that everyone involved has immediate access to important documents, presentations, or spreadsheets.

Step-by-Step Guide:

1. **Create or Open a Google Calendar Event**:

   o   Open Google Calendar and select the date for your event.

   o   Click the "Create" button to start a new event or edit an existing one.

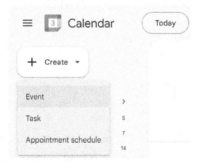

2. **Locate the Attachment Option**:

   o   In the event creation window, find the paperclip icon labeled "Add attachment."

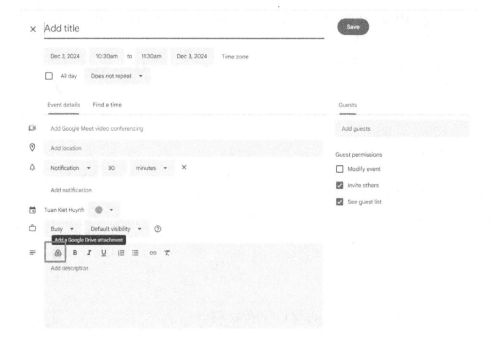

3. **Attach Files from Google Drive**:

   o Click on "Add attachment" and select "Google Drive."

   o Browse your Google Drive for the desired file, or use the search bar to find it quickly.

   o Select the file(s) and click "Insert."

4. **Adjust Permissions**:

   o After attaching the file, check the sharing permissions to ensure attendees can view or edit it as needed. Google Calendar will prompt you to update permissions if necessary.

5. **Save the Event**:

   o Once all details and files are added, click "Save" to finalize your event.

Use Case Example:

Imagine scheduling a team meeting to discuss quarterly performance. Attach a Google Sheet containing sales data and a Google Doc outlining discussion points. Attendees can review these files beforehand, leading to a more productive meeting.

Embedding Google Drive Files in Reminders

Google Calendar allows you to set reminders for tasks or deadlines. Linking relevant Google Drive files to these reminders can further enhance your productivity.

How to Link Files to Reminders:

- Create a reminder for a specific task, such as "Submit project report."

- Include the relevant file's URL in the description box.

- When the reminder notification pops up, the file link will be readily available.

Adding Meeting Agendas via Google Docs

A common use case for this integration is creating detailed meeting agendas and attaching them to calendar invites. Here's how:

1. Create a Google Doc with your meeting agenda.

2. Share the document with appropriate permissions (e.g., view or edit).

3. Attach the document to the calendar event as described earlier.

This ensures all attendees can access the agenda beforehand, contributing to a focused and efficient meeting.

Syncing Events with Google Drive for Backup

Google Drive can also serve as a backup repository for your calendar data. By exporting your Google Calendar and storing it on Drive, you ensure your schedule is safe and accessible even if you lose access to your calendar temporarily.

Steps to Export and Store Calendar Data:

1. Go to Google Calendar's settings.

2. Navigate to "Import & Export" and select "Export."

3. Save the exported file (in .ics format) to your Google Drive.

This can be particularly useful for businesses needing to archive schedules or individuals switching between calendar tools.

Best Practices for Using Google Drive and Calendar Together

To maximize the integration between Google Drive and Google Calendar, consider the following tips:

1. **Keep Files Organized**:

   Store event-related files in specific folders on Google Drive. For example, create a "Meeting Materials" folder and subfolders for each meeting or project.

2. **Use Descriptive Names**:

   Clearly name your files to make them easier to find when attaching them to events.

3. **Set Notifications for Shared Files**:

   Enable notifications for shared files to stay updated when collaborators make changes.

4. **Integrate Add-Ons**:

   Use third-party add-ons to enhance the functionality of Google Drive and Calendar, such as tools for project management or workflow automation.

5. **Review Permissions Regularly**:

   Periodically review file permissions to ensure access is granted only to necessary individuals.

Collaborative Use Cases for Teams

1. **Project Kickoff Meetings**: Attach project briefs, timelines, and team rosters from Google Drive to your kickoff event in Google Calendar.

2. **Client Presentations**: Include Google Slides presentations directly in calendar invites for client meetings.

3. **Training Sessions**: Share training materials, such as PDFs or videos stored on Google Drive, with participants via the calendar event.

Conclusion

Integrating Google Drive with Google Calendar is a simple yet powerful way to enhance your workflow. By linking files, creating centralized access points, and fostering collaboration, you can save time and ensure seamless communication within your team or personal schedule. This integration is an indispensable tool for anyone looking to boost productivity and streamline their digital life.

5.3 Version History and Recovery

5.3.1 Viewing File History

Version history is one of the most valuable features of Google Drive, particularly for those working on collaborative projects or managing evolving documents. This functionality ensures that every change made to a file is recorded, allowing users to track edits, identify contributors, and even revert to previous versions if necessary. In this section, we'll walk through the key elements of viewing file history in Google Drive.

What is Version History?

Version history is a timeline of changes made to a file stored on Google Drive. It captures every save point, noting who made each change and when. This feature applies to Google Docs, Sheets, Slides, and other Google Workspace files. For non-Google file types, such as PDFs or images, Drive retains only the latest version unless explicitly uploaded as a new file.

The key benefits of version history include:

- **Transparency**: See a clear record of changes and identify contributors.

- **Accountability**: Track edits and ensure everyone is on the same page.

- **Recovery**: Restore previous versions if something is accidentally deleted or altered.

Accessing Version History

To view a file's version history:

1. **Open the File**: Start by opening the document, spreadsheet, or presentation in the corresponding Google Workspace tool.

2. **Navigate to Version History**:

   o   Click on **File** in the top menu.

- o Select **Version history** from the dropdown menu.

- o Click **See version history**.
  Alternatively, you can use the shortcut Ctrl + Alt + Shift + H (Windows) or Cmd + Option + Shift + H (Mac).

3. **View Changes**: A panel will appear on the right side of the screen, displaying a list of saved versions with timestamps.

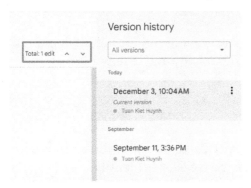

Each entry in the version history shows a snapshot of the file at a specific point in time. Major edits are typically marked as distinct versions, while minor changes may be grouped together.

Understanding the Version History Interface

The version history panel offers a straightforward interface:

- **Timeline**: This chronological list displays each version, including the date and time it was saved. In collaborative files, it also shows the name of the contributor who made the change.

- **Color Coding**: Changes made by different users are highlighted in unique colors, making it easy to distinguish individual contributions.

- **Expand Details**: Click the dropdown arrow next to a version to see sub-versions, which represent incremental changes within a major save point.

Navigating and Reviewing Changes

Once you've opened the version history:

1. **Select a Version**: Click on any entry to view that specific version of the file.

2. **Highlight Changes**: Google Drive automatically highlights edits made in the selected version, such as added or deleted text, formatting adjustments, or inserted comments.

3. **Compare Versions**: Move between versions to compare differences and gain a better understanding of the file's evolution.

For collaborative projects, this feature is particularly useful for identifying when specific edits were made and by whom, fostering accountability and teamwork.

Renaming and Saving Key Versions

In some cases, you might want to preserve specific versions for future reference. Google Drive allows you to rename versions to make them easier to identify:

1. Hover over the version in the timeline.

2. Click the **three-dot menu** (⋮) that appears.

3. Select **Name this version**.

4. Enter a descriptive name, such as "Initial Draft" or "Final Presentation."

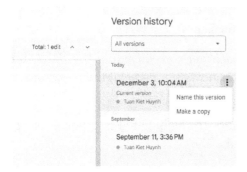

Named versions are not automatically overwritten by subsequent edits, making them a reliable backup for key milestones.

Using Version History for Collaboration

For teams, version history is a powerful tool for ensuring seamless collaboration:

- **Reverting Changes**: If a team member makes unintended edits, the team can quickly revert to a prior version without disrupting workflow.

- **Tracking Progress**: Use the version history to monitor progress on a project, ensuring deadlines and objectives are met.

- **Resolving Conflicts**: In cases of conflicting edits or duplicate work, version history helps teams identify and address issues efficiently.

Practical Tips for Using Version History

1. **Frequent Saves**: Google Drive automatically saves changes, but it's a good habit to pause after significant edits and let Drive register a new save point.

2. **Collaborator Communication**: Encourage team members to add comments or notes alongside their edits, providing context that can be reviewed in version history.

3. **Monitor Edits Regularly**: For large teams or high-stakes projects, regularly check the version history to ensure consistency and quality.

Scenarios Where Version History Shines

- **Undoing Mistakes**: If you accidentally delete a paragraph or overwrite a formula, version history lets you retrieve the lost content instantly.

- **Academic Projects**: Track changes to a shared group assignment and identify contributors for grading purposes.

- **Corporate Workflows**: Monitor edits to contracts or proposals, ensuring every change is documented and approved.

Limitations of Version History

While version history is an incredibly useful feature, it has some limitations:

- **Storage Impact**: Extensive version history may take up additional storage for large files.

- **Non-Google Files**: For non-Google file types, Drive doesn't maintain a detailed version history. To track changes, you'll need to manually upload new versions.

- **Irreversible Deletions**: If a file is permanently deleted from Drive, its version history is also lost.

By mastering version history, users can unlock a critical aspect of Google Drive's functionality, ensuring better collaboration, stronger accountability, and enhanced file management. Whether you're managing a solo project or working with a team, this feature ensures you never lose track of your work's evolution.

5.3.2 Restoring Previous Versions

One of the most reassuring features of Google Drive is the ability to restore previous versions of files. This capability allows users to retrieve earlier versions of documents, spreadsheets, or presentations in case of accidental changes, deletions, or if they wish to revisit an earlier draft. This section will guide you through the process, explain its importance, and highlight some practical scenarios where restoring previous versions can be a lifesaver.

Why Restore Previous Versions?

Google Drive's version history feature ensures that every change made to a file is tracked and can be undone if needed. This functionality is particularly valuable for:

1. **Accidental Modifications:** Mistakenly deleted a paragraph or overwrote an important calculation? Version history ensures those changes aren't permanent.

2. **Collaboration Challenges:** In collaborative environments, multiple contributors might make conflicting edits. Restoring a previous version can resolve disputes or restore coherence.

3. **Experimentation:** Working on a creative project or complex data analysis? You can experiment freely, knowing you can always revert to an earlier, more polished version.

4. **Data Recovery:** In cases of file corruption or unexpected errors, previous versions act as a safeguard against data loss.

How to Access Version History

Before restoring a file to a previous version, you need to understand how to view version history:

1. **Open the File:** Navigate to the file you want to inspect and open it in its respective Google app (Docs, Sheets, or Slides).

2. **Access Version History:**

   o   Click on **File** in the menu bar.

   o   Select **Version History** > **See Version History** (shortcut: Ctrl+Alt+Shift+H for Windows or Cmd+Option+Shift+H for Mac).

3. **Explore Versions:** A sidebar will appear on the right, listing all saved versions of the file. Each entry is timestamped, and if you hover over a version, you'll see the user who made the changes.

Steps to Restore a Previous Version

Once you've identified the version you want to restore, follow these steps:

1. **Select the Version:** Click on the desired version in the sidebar to preview it. Google Drive highlights changes compared to the current version, making it easy to verify.

2. **Restore the Version:**

   o   Click the **Restore This Version** button at the top of the screen.

   o   Confirm your action in the pop-up dialog box.

- o The restored version becomes the latest version of the file, but all subsequent edits remain in the version history for further restoration if needed.

3. **Optional - Make a Copy Before Restoring:**

   - o If you don't want to overwrite the current version, click on the **More Actions** menu (three dots) next to the version and select **Make a Copy**.

   - o The selected version will be saved as a separate file in your Google Drive, allowing you to preserve both versions.

Best Practices for Using Version History

To maximize the benefits of version history and restoration, follow these best practices:

1. **Name Important Versions:** Use the "Name this version" option in the version history panel to label significant drafts or milestones. For instance, "Initial Draft," "Final Presentation," or "Reviewed by Manager."

2. **Communicate in Collaborative Projects:** Inform collaborators before restoring a previous version to avoid confusion.

3. **Regularly Check Version History:** In ongoing projects, periodically review version history to ensure key changes are documented and recoverable.

4. **Combine Changes if Needed:** After restoring, you can copy elements from different versions into the restored file to merge useful updates.

Practical Scenarios of Version Restoration

Here are some real-life examples to demonstrate how restoring previous versions can be invaluable:

- **Academic Projects:** A student accidentally deletes several pages of their thesis while editing late at night. Version history allows them to restore the document to the version saved earlier that day.

- **Team Collaboration:** In a shared marketing presentation, one contributor mistakenly removes a key slide. Restoring the version from before the deletion ensures no content is lost.

- **Budget Analysis:** An accountant realizes that an earlier formula in a financial spreadsheet was more accurate. By restoring an older version, they save time recalculating.

- **Creative Writing:** An author experimenting with different storylines can revert to an earlier draft if they decide to pursue a different narrative path.

Limitations of Version History and How to Address Them

While the version history feature is robust, it does have some limitations:

1. **Storage Duration:** Version history isn't retained indefinitely for all file types. For non-Google formats like PDFs or images, previous versions may be deleted after 30 days or 100 versions.

   o **Solution:** Regularly export important versions or convert files to Google's native formats (Docs, Sheets, Slides).

2. **File Size:** Large files may encounter slower loading times when reviewing version history.

   o **Solution:** Optimize file size or work with smaller chunks where possible.

3. **User Error:** Restoring a version by mistake could overwrite recent updates.

   o **Solution:** Always review the version thoroughly before restoration and communicate with collaborators.

Pro Tips for Efficient Restoration .

1. **Utilize Keyboard Shortcuts:** Master shortcuts like Ctrl+Alt+Shift+H to quickly access version history.

2. **Leverage Google Drive's Backup Feature:** Enable backup settings for critical folders, adding an extra layer of protection.

3. **Integrate with Add-Ons:** Tools like Revision History Analytics can help you visualize complex version histories for large projects.

Conclusion

The ability to restore previous versions is one of Google Drive's standout features, empowering users to safeguard their work and recover from errors effortlessly. By understanding the steps and best practices outlined in this section, you can confidently navigate version history and ensure your projects stay on track, no matter the challenges you face.

In the next section, we'll explore **Chapter 6: Security and Privacy**, where you'll learn how to protect your files and manage permissions effectively.

CHAPTER VI
Security and Privacy

6.1 Understanding Google Drive Security Features

Google Drive provides a robust set of security features designed to protect your data, ensuring it is safe, accessible, and manageable. This chapter will delve into the key security functionalities of Google Drive, focusing on the mechanisms that safeguard your files from unauthorized access and cyber threats.

6.1.1 Two-Factor Authentication

Two-Factor Authentication (2FA), also known as two-step verification, is one of the most effective security measures you can enable to protect your Google Drive account. It adds an additional layer of security beyond your password, ensuring that even if someone gains access to your credentials, they cannot log into your account without the second factor.

What is Two-Factor Authentication?

Two-factor authentication combines two independent forms of verification to confirm your identity:

1. **Something You Know**: Your password.

2. **Something You Have**: A physical device, such as your smartphone or a security key.

This dual approach minimizes the risks associated with compromised passwords, which are often targeted through phishing attacks, data breaches, or weak password practices.

How Does Two-Factor Authentication Work in Google Drive?

When you enable 2FA for your Google Account, each login attempt triggers a second verification step. Here's how the process typically works:

1. Enter your Google Account username and password as usual.

2. A second prompt requires you to provide an additional piece of evidence, such as:

   o A code sent to your registered mobile number via SMS.

   o A code generated by an authenticator app, such as Google Authenticator.

   o Approval of a login attempt through a notification sent to your mobile device.

   o The use of a physical security key, such as a YubiKey.

Only after both steps are successfully completed will you gain access to your Google Drive and other Google services.

Setting Up Two-Factor Authentication

Follow these steps to enable 2FA for your Google Account:

1. Log in to your Google Account.

2. Go to **Security Settings** by navigating to *My Account > Security*.

3. Find the option labeled **2-Step Verification** and click **Get Started**.

4. Google will guide you through the setup process, including:

   o Verifying your phone number.

   o Choosing a primary method for receiving codes (e.g., SMS, Google Authenticator).

   o Optionally setting up backup methods, such as security keys or backup codes.

Once 2FA is enabled, you can adjust settings or add more methods through the same interface.

Types of Two-Factor Authentication Supported by Google Drive

Google offers several methods for completing the second verification step:

1. **SMS Codes**:

Google sends a unique six-digit code to your registered mobile number. While convenient, SMS codes are less secure than other methods, as they can be intercepted via SIM swapping or malware.

2. **Authenticator Apps**:

Apps like Google Authenticator or Authy generate time-based one-time passwords (TOTP) that are valid for a limited time. This method is more secure than SMS and works offline.

3. **Google Prompts**:

When you attempt to log in, Google sends a push notification to your registered mobile device. You can approve or deny the request with a single tap. This method is both secure and user-friendly.

4. **Security Keys**:

A hardware-based option, security keys are USB or NFC devices that verify your identity when plugged into or tapped on your device. They are highly secure and resistant to phishing.

5. **Backup Codes**:

Google provides a set of backup codes that you can print or save for emergencies, such as losing your phone. Each code can be used once.

Benefits of Two-Factor Authentication

1. **Enhanced Security**: Even if your password is stolen, attackers cannot access your account without the second factor.

2. **Protection Against Phishing**: 2FA helps prevent unauthorized access even if you accidentally disclose your password.

3. **Flexibility**: Multiple verification methods allow you to choose what works best for your needs.

4. **Peace of Mind**: Knowing that an extra layer of security protects your files ensures greater confidence in using Google Drive for personal or professional purposes.

Challenges and How to Overcome Them

While 2FA significantly enhances security, it is not without challenges:

1. **Losing Access to Your Second Factor**:
   If you lose your phone or security key, it may be difficult to access your account. To mitigate this:

   - Set up multiple verification methods.

   - Keep backup codes in a secure location.

   - Ensure your recovery email and phone number are up to date.

2. **Device Compatibility**:

   Some older devices or browsers may not support certain 2FA methods. Use modern hardware and software for compatibility.

3. **Convenience vs. Security**:

   Some users may find 2FA cumbersome. However, the added security outweighs the minor inconvenience. Enable Google Prompts for a more seamless experience.

Best Practices for Two-Factor Authentication

To maximize the benefits of 2FA:

- Regularly review and update your authentication methods.

- Avoid relying solely on SMS codes; consider using Google Authenticator or a security key.

- Enable 2FA for all accounts linked to your Google Drive, such as email and cloud services.

- Monitor login activity through your Google Account settings to detect unauthorized attempts.

Conclusion

Two-Factor Authentication is a powerful tool in Google Drive's security arsenal. By enabling this feature, you can significantly reduce the risk of unauthorized access to your account. While it requires a few extra steps during login, the peace of mind and protection it offers are well worth the effort. The next section will explore another critical security feature: encryption basics, which ensures that your data remains safe during storage and transmission.

6.1.2 Encryption Basics

Encryption is a cornerstone of modern data security, ensuring that the information you store in Google Drive remains protected from unauthorized access. By understanding how encryption works and how Google Drive implements it, you can feel more confident about the safety of your files.

What Is Encryption?

Encryption is the process of converting readable data, known as plaintext, into an unreadable format called ciphertext. This transformation ensures that only authorized parties with the correct decryption key can access the original data. In simpler terms, encryption acts as a digital lock for your files, safeguarding them from prying eyes.

Google Drive employs encryption at various stages to protect your data:

1. **In Transit**: This occurs when your files are being uploaded to or downloaded from Google Drive.

2. **At Rest**: This applies to files stored on Google's servers.

Encryption in Transit

When you access Google Drive from your web browser, mobile app, or third-party integrations, the data transmitted between your device and Google's servers is encrypted using Transport Layer Security (TLS). TLS creates a secure tunnel for your data, protecting it from interception by hackers, even when you're on an unsecured network, such as public Wi-Fi.

Key Features of Encryption in Transit:

- **Automatic Protection**: TLS encryption is enabled by default, so you don't need to configure any settings.

- **End-to-End Security**: This ensures data integrity and prevents tampering during transmission.

- **Compatibility with Modern Browsers**: Most modern web browsers support TLS, ensuring seamless connectivity.

Encryption at Rest

Once your files reach Google's servers, they are encrypted again to protect them from unauthorized access within Google's infrastructure. This process is known as encryption at rest. Google Drive uses Advanced Encryption Standard (AES) with 256-bit keys for this purpose, a widely recognized and robust encryption method.

Key Benefits of Encryption at Rest:

- **Data Privacy**: Your files are inaccessible to anyone without the proper authentication.

- **Compliance**: AES-256 meets global security standards, making Google Drive suitable for storing sensitive information.

- **Layered Security**: In addition to encryption, Google's servers are protected by physical and digital safeguards.

The Role of Keys in Encryption

Encryption relies on keys to secure and unlock data. Google Drive manages encryption keys securely within its infrastructure:

- **Key Management**: Keys are stored in a separate, highly secure location, minimizing the risk of exposure.

- **Rotating Keys**: Encryption keys are periodically rotated to maintain security integrity.

Additional Security Measures

Google Drive doesn't stop at encryption. It integrates additional safeguards to ensure a secure user experience:

- **File Integrity Checks**: Regular checks verify that your files haven't been altered or corrupted.

- **Access Monitoring**: Activity logs allow you to track who accessed your files and when, adding an extra layer of accountability.

Advantages of Google Drive's Encryption System

1. **Seamless Integration**: Encryption occurs automatically, requiring no additional effort on your part.

2. **Comprehensive Coverage**: Both in-transit and at-rest encryption ensures end-to-end data protection.

3. **Adaptability**: Google's encryption methods are continually updated to combat emerging security threats.

Limitations and Considerations

While encryption significantly enhances security, it's not foolproof:

- **User Responsibility**: If your account credentials are compromised, encryption won't prevent unauthorized access.

- **Government Requests**: Google may be legally required to decrypt and share data with authorities, though this is limited to specific cases.

Best Practices for Leveraging Encryption

To maximize the benefits of Google Drive's encryption features, consider the following:

- **Enable Two-Factor Authentication (2FA)**: Combine encryption with 2FA for enhanced security.

- **Avoid Public Wi-Fi for Sensitive Files**: While encryption in transit protects your data, using a secure network reduces risks further.

- **Regularly Monitor File Activity**: Check activity logs to identify any unauthorized attempts to access your files.

Beyond Encryption: Taking Additional Steps

Encryption is a powerful tool, but combining it with proactive security measures can provide comprehensive protection. These include managing file access permissions (discussed in 6.2) and implementing strong account passwords.

By understanding encryption basics and its implementation in Google Drive, you can better appreciate the platform's dedication to keeping your data safe. As technology evolves, Google continues to enhance its encryption protocols, ensuring your files remain protected against ever-changing security threats.

6.2 Managing File Access Permissions

Managing file access permissions is one of the most essential aspects of using Google Drive, especially for users who frequently share documents with colleagues, friends, or collaborators. Properly understanding and utilizing permissions not only ensures your files are shared with the intended people but also protects sensitive information from unauthorized access. In this section, we'll dive deep into the mechanics of file permissions, explain the different levels of access, and provide best practices for managing shared content effectively.

Understanding Permission Levels

Google Drive provides several levels of access permissions that determine what collaborators can do with a shared file or folder. These include:

1. **Viewer**:

    o This is the most restricted level of access.

    o A person with "Viewer" permission can only view the content but cannot make any changes.

    o Ideal for files that contain finalized content, such as reports or presentations, where you want feedback but no alterations.

2. **Commenter**:

    o Allows the recipient to add comments or suggestions but not edit the file directly.

    o Useful when collaborating on drafts where input is needed without changing the original content.

3. **Editor**:

    o Grants full editing rights, enabling the user to make changes to the content.

o   This is ideal for team projects where everyone is responsible for contributing and modifying the file.

4. **Owner**:

    o   The highest level of control is reserved for the file owner, who can transfer ownership, delete files, or change permissions for other collaborators.

    o   Ownership should only be transferred when you no longer need to manage the document.

How to Change Permissions

Adjusting permissions is straightforward in Google Drive. Follow these steps to ensure the right people have access:

1. **Open the Share Dialog**:

    o   Right-click on the file or folder you want to share and select "Share." Alternatively, select the file and click the "Share" icon in the toolbar.

2. **Add Collaborators**:

    o   Enter the email addresses of the people you want to share the file with.

    o   Use the dropdown menu next to each name to assign the appropriate level of access (Viewer, Commenter, or Editor).

3. **Set Link Sharing Options**:

    o   You can share files via a link and control who can access it.

    o   Options include:

        ▪   **Restricted**: Only people you've explicitly shared the file with can access it.

        ▪   **Anyone with the link**: Anyone who has the link can view, comment, or edit the file, depending on the permission level you set.

4. **Adjust Advanced Settings**:

    o   Click on the gear icon in the share dialog for additional controls, such as:

        ▪   Disabling download, print, or copy options for viewers and commenters.

        ▪   Preventing editors from adding new collaborators.

5. **Save Changes**:

    o   After setting the permissions, click "Done" to save your changes.

Using Shared Drives

For teams or organizations using Google Workspace, Shared Drives provide an additional layer of permission management.

1. **What Are Shared Drives?**

    o   Files in a Shared Drive belong to the team, not an individual.

    o   Permissions are managed at the folder level, making it easier to collaborate on large projects.

2. **Permission Types in Shared Drives**:

    o   **Manager**: Full access to add members, manage permissions, and edit content.

    o   **Content Manager**: Can add, edit, and move files within the drive.

    o   **Contributor**: Can add files but cannot edit or delete existing ones.

    o   **Viewer/Commenter**: Similar to individual file permissions.

3. **Best Practices for Shared Drives**:

    o   Assign the least amount of access needed for collaborators to complete their tasks.

    o   Regularly review and update permissions to align with team changes.

Common Mistakes and How to Avoid Them

1. **Sharing with the Wrong People**:

   o   Always double-check email addresses before granting access. A small typo can lead to unintended sharing.

2. **Overusing "Anyone with the Link"**:

   o   While convenient, this option can be risky if the link is shared broadly. Use it sparingly and only when absolutely necessary.

3. **Neglecting Permission Reviews**:

   o   Periodically audit who has access to your files. People who no longer need access (e.g., former team members) should be removed.

4. **Forgetting to Adjust Permissions for Sensitive Documents**:

   o   For files containing confidential or sensitive information, always set permissions to "Restricted" and carefully control who can view or edit the content.

Best Practices for Managing File Permissions

1. **Use Groups for Large Teams**:

   o   Instead of adding individual email addresses, create a Google Group and assign permissions to the group. This simplifies permission management as team members join or leave.

2. **Set Expiry Dates for Temporary Access**:

   o   When sharing files with external collaborators, set an expiry date for their access. This ensures they can't view the content indefinitely.

3. **Regularly Audit Shared Files**:

- o Use Google Drive's "Shared with me" and "Shared by me" sections to review all shared files and adjust permissions as needed.

4. **Use Descriptive File and Folder Names**:

- o Clear names make it easier to identify what is being shared, reducing the likelihood of unintentional sharing.

Advanced Permission Management Tools

1. **Google Drive Add-ons and Integrations**:

- o Tools like DocuSign and AODocs can enhance permission control, especially for business users.

2. **Activity Monitor**:

- o Use the Activity Dashboard in Google Drive to track file access and identify any suspicious activity.

3. **Google Workspace Admin Console**:

- o For administrators, the console provides organization-wide control over file permissions and sharing settings.

By mastering file access permissions in Google Drive, you can ensure that your files remain secure and accessible to the right people. Whether you're collaborating on a team project or simply sharing photos with friends, taking the time to understand these features will make your Google Drive experience more efficient and stress-free.

6.3 Tips for Securing Your Account

Securing your Google Drive account is essential to protect not only your files and documents but also your personal data. Given the increasing reliance on cloud storage services, the potential risks of cyberattacks, and the growing number of online threats, it is crucial to take proactive steps to safeguard your Google Drive account. This section will outline key tips to help you secure your account and ensure your data remains private and protected.

Use a Strong Password

The first and most obvious step in securing your Google Drive account is using a strong and unique password. A weak password is one of the most common vulnerabilities hackers exploit to gain unauthorized access to accounts. To create a robust password, follow these guidelines:

1. **Length**: A strong password should be at least 12 characters long. The longer the password, the harder it is for hackers to guess or crack.

2. **Complexity**: Use a combination of uppercase and lowercase letters, numbers, and special characters (such as @, #, $, %, etc.). This makes the password harder for automated tools to break.

3. **Avoid Common Words**: Do not use easily guessable words like your name, birthdate, or simple dictionary words. Instead, use a random sequence of characters.

4. **Use a Password Manager**: Managing strong, unique passwords for every account can be challenging. A password manager can securely store your passwords and help you generate strong ones, ensuring you don't use the same password across multiple accounts.

By adhering to these password practices, you can significantly reduce the likelihood of someone gaining access to your Google Drive account.

Enable Two-Factor Authentication (2FA)

As discussed earlier, enabling Two-Factor Authentication (2FA) is one of the most effective ways to enhance the security of your Google Drive account. 2FA adds an additional layer of protection by requiring something you know (your password) and something you have (a verification code sent to your phone or generated by an authentication app) to access your account.

Here's how to enable 2FA for Google Drive:

1. **Go to your Google Account Settings**: Start by signing in to your Google Account. Then navigate to your account settings.

2. **Select Security**: In the left-hand sidebar, click on "Security."

3. **Enable 2-Step Verification**: Scroll down to the "Signing in to Google" section and click on "2-Step Verification."

4. **Follow the prompts**: Google will guide you through the process, where you'll choose how you'd like to receive your verification code. You can opt for SMS, use the Google Authenticator app, or enable Google prompts to get notifications on your mobile device.

Once 2FA is enabled, you'll need to enter a verification code every time you log in to your Google Drive account. This means that even if someone manages to steal your password, they won't be able to access your account without the second factor.

Review Account Activity Regularly

One of the best ways to catch any suspicious activity early is by regularly reviewing your account activity. Google provides tools to help you track all actions performed on your Google Drive account. To monitor your account activity:

1. **Check Recent Activity**: Sign in to your Google account and go to the "Security" section. Look for the "Recent Security Events" and "Your Devices" sections. These will show any unusual activity, such as sign-ins from unfamiliar devices or locations.

2. **Review File Access Logs**: You can also check who has accessed your files and folders in Google Drive. For shared files, Google Drive allows you to see when someone views or edits a document. If you notice any unknown users or suspicious actions, immediately revoke their access or change your sharing settings.

3. **Set Up Security Alerts**: Google offers security alerts for unusual login attempts, such as logging in from a new device or location. You can enable these alerts to be notified immediately if something unusual occurs.

By regularly monitoring your Google Drive account, you can detect potential threats before they escalate into major security issues.

Be Cautious with Third-Party Apps

Many users integrate third-party applications with their Google Drive accounts to extend functionality, such as for productivity, file management, or cloud storage. However, giving third-party apps access to your Google Drive can expose your files to unnecessary risks, especially if those apps have weak security practices.

To keep your Google Drive account safe, consider the following:

1. **Review Connected Apps**: Regularly review the third-party apps that have access to your Google Drive account. Go to your Google Account settings, click on "Security," and then select "Third-party apps with account access." Here you can see which apps are connected to your Google Drive account.

2. **Revoke Access**: If you no longer use a third-party app or don't trust it, revoke its access immediately. This will prevent it from accessing your Google Drive files. You can do this from the same page where you reviewed connected apps.

3. **Be Mindful of Permissions**: When you give an app access to your Google Drive, make sure to only grant the minimum permissions necessary for the app to function. Don't give apps more access than they need.

It's also important to install apps only from trusted sources, such as the official Google Workspace Marketplace. Avoid downloading apps from unverified developers or websites, as these may be malicious and compromise your account.

Be Wary of Phishing Scams

Phishing is a type of cyberattack where hackers impersonate legitimate services or companies to trick you into revealing your personal information, such as login credentials. Google Drive users are often targeted by phishing scams that attempt to steal their account details or infect their devices with malware.

Here are some tips to protect yourself from phishing attempts:

1. **Check the URL**: Phishing emails often contain links to fake websites that look like the real thing. Always double-check the URL before entering any sensitive information. Google's official websites always start with "https://accounts.google.com" or "https://drive.google.com."

2. **Don't Open Suspicious Links or Attachments**: Be cautious with emails or messages that contain links or attachments, especially if they seem suspicious or unexpected. Even if the email appears to come from someone you know, verify its legitimacy before clicking any links.

3. **Look for Red Flags**: Phishing emails may have poor grammar, spelling mistakes, or generic greetings like "Dear User." They might ask for sensitive information or prompt you to act quickly to resolve an issue.

4. **Enable Google's Anti-Phishing Features**: Google includes anti-phishing features in Gmail and other services, which will flag suspicious emails and warn you if a message might be a phishing attempt. Always heed these warnings.

By staying vigilant and educating yourself about phishing scams, you can prevent falling victim to these attacks.

Protect Your Devices

The security of your Google Drive account isn't just dependent on your account settings; it also relies on the security of the devices you use to access Google Drive. Protecting your devices from malware, unauthorized access, and other risks is crucial.

Here are some tips for securing your devices:

1. **Use Antivirus Software**: Install reputable antivirus software on your devices to help detect and block malware that could compromise your Google Drive account.

2. **Keep Your Software Updated**: Ensure that your operating system, browsers, and apps are up to date with the latest security patches. Software updates often include fixes for vulnerabilities that hackers can exploit.

3. **Lock Your Devices**: Use strong passcodes or biometric authentication (such as fingerprint or face recognition) to lock your devices. This prevents unauthorized individuals from accessing your data if your device is lost or stolen.

4. **Use Virtual Private Networks (VPNs)**: When accessing Google Drive from public or unsecured networks, consider using a VPN to encrypt your internet connection and protect your data from being intercepted.

By following these device security practices, you can further protect your Google Drive account from external threats.

Use File Encryption for Sensitive Data

For highly sensitive files, consider using file encryption in addition to Google Drive's built-in security features. File encryption ensures that even if someone gains access to your files, they cannot read or use them without the encryption key.

There are several third-party encryption tools available that you can use to encrypt your files before uploading them to Google Drive. Some tools even offer password protection for files, adding another layer of security. Ensure you store your encryption keys or passwords securely and separately from your files to avoid losing access.

By following these tips, you can significantly enhance the security of your Google Drive account and ensure that your files and data remain safe from unauthorized access. In today's digital age, taking these proactive steps is essential to maintaining the privacy and integrity of your online information.

CHAPTER VII
Maximizing Productivity with Google Drive

7.1 Keyboard Shortcuts

Mastering keyboard shortcuts is one of the fastest and most effective ways to boost productivity when using Google Drive. These shortcuts not only save time but also enhance efficiency, allowing you to navigate, manage files, and execute commands with minimal effort. In this section, we'll explore the most useful keyboard shortcuts for Google Drive, organized by function, along with tips for incorporating them into your daily workflow.

Navigating the Google Drive Interface

Keyboard shortcuts make it easy to move around Google Drive without touching your mouse. Here are the most common shortcuts for navigation:

- **Switching Between Views**
  - Press **G + L** to open the "List View."
  - Press **G + G** to switch back to the "Grid View."

- **Opening Menus**
  - **Shift + T**: Create a new folder.
  - **Shift + F**: Open the "File" menu.

- **Quick Navigation**
  - **G + N**: Go to the "Notifications" panel.

- o **G + H**: Jump to the "Shared with Me" section.

- o **G + U**: Go to "Recent Files."

Managing Files and Folders

Managing your documents and folders becomes a breeze with these shortcuts:

- **Creating Items**

    - o **Shift + T**: Create a new folder.

    - o **Shift + P**: Create a new document.

    - o **Shift + S**: Create a new spreadsheet.

    - o **Shift + C**: Create a new slide presentation.

- **Selecting Items**

    - o Use the arrow keys to navigate between files.

    - o Press **Spacebar** to preview a file.

    - o Press **X** to select or deselect the currently highlighted file.

- **Moving and Organizing**

    - o **Shift + Z**: Add a file to another folder without moving it.

    - o **Ctrl + X**: Cut a file.

    - o **Ctrl + V**: Paste a file into a folder.

Searching and Filtering Files

Google Drive's search functionality is powerful, and with shortcuts, you can quickly locate files.

- **Search Command**:

    - o Press **/ (forward slash)** to jump to the search bar.

    - o Enter keywords to filter results.

- **Refining Searches**:

- o **Ctrl + F**: Search within the current folder.

- o Use search operators like "type:pdf" or "owner:me" for advanced filtering.

File Actions

Quickly perform actions on files without opening additional menus:

- **Opening and Previewing Files**

  - o **Enter**: Open the selected file.

  - o **Spacebar**: Preview the file in a pop-up.

- **Renaming Files**

  - o Select the file and press **N** to rename it.

- **Deleting and Restoring Files**

  - o Press **Delete** to move the selected file to the trash.

  - o To restore a file, navigate to the "Trash" section and press **Shift + R** on the selected file.

- **Downloading Files**

  - o Highlight the file and press **Shift + D** to download it.

Collaborative Features

Google Drive's collaboration features shine with keyboard shortcuts that streamline teamwork:

- **Commenting on Files**

  - o Highlight text in a document and press **Ctrl + Alt + M** to add a comment.

- **Sharing Files**

  - o Select a file and press **Ctrl + S** to open the sharing menu.

  - o Use arrow keys to navigate sharing options.

General Productivity Tips

- **Combining Shortcuts**

  Combine multiple shortcuts for a smoother workflow. For example, after opening a file with **Enter**, use **Ctrl + P** to print directly.

- **Practicing Regularly**

  Familiarize yourself with a few shortcuts at a time. Start with basic navigation and file actions, then add more advanced commands as you go.

- **Creating a Cheat Sheet**

  If you're new to shortcuts, print a cheat sheet and keep it handy for quick reference.

7.1.7 Accessibility and Customization

Google Drive offers additional options to customize shortcuts or enhance accessibility:

- **Enabling Accessibility Features**

  If you rely on screen readers, ensure Google Drive's accessibility settings are enabled.

- **Customizing Shortcuts**

  Currently, Google Drive doesn't support shortcut customization directly, but browser extensions like **AutoHotkey** can help.

Keyboard shortcuts transform Google Drive into a powerful productivity tool. By investing time in mastering these commands, you can reduce repetitive actions, speed up daily tasks, and focus on what truly matters: getting work done.

7.2 Using Google Drive on Mobile Devices

7.2.1 Navigating the Mobile App

The Google Drive mobile app is a powerful tool that allows users to manage files, collaborate with others, and stay productive while on the go. Available for both Android and iOS devices, the app offers a streamlined experience with an interface designed for touchscreens. In this section, we'll explore the app's layout, key features, and best practices for efficient navigation.

1. Downloading and Installing the App

Before diving into the app's interface, ensure it is installed on your mobile device. To download Google Drive:

- For **Android users**, visit the Google Play Store, search for "Google Drive," and tap *Install*.

- For **iOS users**, head to the App Store, search for "Google Drive," and tap *Get*.

Once installed, open the app and sign in with your Google account credentials. If you have multiple accounts, you can switch between them within the app.

2. The Home Screen

Upon launching Google Drive, you'll arrive at the **Home screen**, which provides a snapshot of your most recent and important files. The layout includes:

- **Search Bar:** Located at the top, this is your gateway to finding specific files or folders. Use keywords or filters to refine your search.

- **Quick Access Panel:** Below the search bar, you'll see thumbnails of recently opened or edited files for easy access.

- **Folders and Files:** Scroll down to browse through files and folders stored in your drive. These are typically sorted by last modified date, but you can customize this order.

- **Floating Action Button (FAB):** A circular button (often with a plus sign) located in the lower-right corner. Tapping this opens options for creating new files, uploading content, or scanning documents.

3. Navigating the Sidebar Menu

The sidebar menu, accessed by tapping the three horizontal lines (often called the "hamburger menu") in the top-left corner, provides shortcuts to key sections of the app:

- **My Drive:** Your primary storage area where all files and folders reside.

- **Shared with Me:** A collection of files and folders that others have shared with you.

- **Starred:** Quick access to files and folders you've marked as important.

- **Offline:** Displays files you've made available for offline access.

- **Trash:** A temporary holding area for deleted files. Items here can be permanently deleted or restored.

- **Storage:** View how much storage space you've used and purchase more if needed.

4. Understanding File and Folder Actions

Tapping on any file or folder brings up options for interacting with it. These include:

- **Previewing Files:** Tap once to open and view the file. For Google Docs, Sheets, and Slides, you can edit directly within the app.

- **Menu Options:** Tap the three dots next to a file or folder to reveal actions such as *Share*, *Move*, *Rename*, or *Download*.

- **Dragging and Dropping:** On some devices, you can long-press on a file or folder to drag it into a new location.

5. Creating and Uploading Files

Using the Floating Action Button, you can:

- **Create New Files:** Start a Google Doc, Sheet, or Slide directly within the app. You can also create folders to keep files organized.

- **Upload Files and Folders:** Select files from your device to upload them to Google Drive. This is particularly useful for backing up photos or transferring documents.

- **Scan Documents:** Use your device's camera to scan physical documents. Google Drive converts these scans into PDF files for easy storage and sharing.

6. Managing Files Offline

One of the most useful features of the mobile app is the ability to work offline. To make a file available offline:

- Locate the file in your drive.

- Tap the three-dot menu next to it.

- Select *Make Available Offline.*

Offline files are stored locally on your device and can be accessed even without an internet connection. Any changes made to these files will sync automatically once you're back online.

7. Collaboration and Sharing on Mobile

The Google Drive app simplifies collaboration, enabling you to share files and folders directly from your device.

- **Sharing a File:** Tap the three-dot menu next to a file, select *Share*, and enter the email addresses of the recipients. You can also adjust permissions (e.g., viewer, commenter, editor).

- **Adding Comments:** Open a document, highlight a section, and tap the comment icon to add notes or feedback.

The app also supports real-time collaboration, meaning multiple users can view or edit a document simultaneously.

8. Customizing Settings

To tailor the app to your needs, explore the settings menu:

- **Notifications:** Turn on notifications to receive updates about shared files or collaboration activity.

- **Theme:** Switch between light and dark mode for a more comfortable viewing experience.

- **Data Usage:** Adjust settings to limit data usage, such as restricting uploads to Wi-Fi only.

9. Advanced Tips for Mobile Navigation

To maximize your productivity, consider these tips:

- **Pin Frequently Used Files:** Mark important files as "Starred" for quick access.

- **Use Voice Commands:** On Android devices, you can use Google Assistant to open files or search your Drive.

- **Search Filters:** Use advanced filters, such as file type or date modified, to locate specific files quickly.

- **Integration with Other Apps:** Open files directly in other Google apps like Docs or Sheets for seamless editing.

10. Troubleshooting Common Issues

If you encounter problems with the mobile app:

- **File Syncing Issues:** Ensure you have a stable internet connection and check your sync settings.

- **App Crashes or Freezes:** Restart your device or update the app to the latest version.

- **Storage Limits:** Review your storage usage in the *Storage* section and delete unnecessary files to free up space.

Conclusion

Navigating the Google Drive mobile app is intuitive once you understand its layout and features. Whether you're uploading files, collaborating on documents, or accessing files offline, the app is designed to keep you productive no matter where you are. By mastering the tips and tools outlined above, you can unlock the full potential of Google Drive on your mobile device.

7.2.2 Uploading Files on the Go

Google Drive's mobile app offers unparalleled convenience for uploading files directly from your smartphone or tablet. Whether you're saving a document on the fly, backing up important media, or transferring files for work, understanding how to effectively use the app's upload features can significantly boost your productivity. This section will guide you step-by-step through the process, ensuring you can effortlessly upload files while on the move.

Why Upload Files on the Go?

In today's fast-paced world, the ability to upload files directly from your mobile device is not just a luxury but a necessity. Here are a few scenarios where mobile uploads are especially useful:

- **Capturing and Saving Memories:** Instantly upload photos and videos to your Drive after an event or trip to ensure they're securely backed up.

- **Sharing Work Documents:** Need to send a signed contract or a scanned receipt to your team? The mobile app makes it seamless.

- **Accessing Files Across Devices:** Upload files from your phone to access them later on your laptop or desktop.

- **Minimizing Device Storage Use:** Transfer large files from your phone to the cloud to free up space.

Step-by-Step Guide to Uploading Files

Uploading files to Google Drive on your mobile device is simple and intuitive. Let's explore the process for both Android and iOS platforms.

Step 1: Open the Google Drive App

Ensure the app is installed on your device and signed in with the appropriate Google account. Navigate to your desired folder or the root directory where you want to store the file.

Step 2: Tap the "+" Button

In the bottom-right corner of the app, you'll find a circular "+" icon. Tap this to open a menu of options, including "Upload."

Step 3: Choose Your File

- For **Photos and Videos**: Select the "Upload" option and choose files from your device's gallery. You can upload one or multiple items at once.

- For **Documents**: Navigate to the file location using the built-in file browser. Select the document you wish to upload.

- For **Other File Types**: Tap "Browse" to access other apps or folders, such as downloads or email attachments.

Step 4: Monitor Upload Progress

After selecting your file, it will begin uploading. A status bar will appear at the bottom of the screen to track progress. You can continue using the app while uploads are in progress.

Step 5: Confirm Upload Completion

Once the upload is complete, the file will appear in your selected folder. Tap on it to verify that it opens correctly.

Tips for Efficient Mobile Uploads

To make the most of Google Drive's mobile upload functionality, consider these practical tips:

1. **Optimize File Sizes**

   Large files can slow down uploads, especially on limited data connections. Use apps to compress files before uploading them.

2. **Leverage Wi-Fi Connections**

   Uploading over Wi-Fi is typically faster and won't consume your mobile data. Turn on the "Wi-Fi Only" option in the app settings to prevent accidental data usage.

3. **Organize Your Files Before Uploading**

   Decide on a clear folder structure to keep your Drive organized. Upload files directly to the appropriate folders rather than sorting them later.

4. **Batch Uploads for Efficiency**

   Instead of uploading files one by one, select multiple files at once for batch uploading. This feature saves time and ensures consistency.

5. **Enable Offline Mode**

   If you're in an area with poor internet connectivity, upload files when online and mark them for offline access so they're readily available even without a connection.

Common Upload Scenarios and Solutions

Scenario 1: Uploading Photos and Videos

Imagine you're on vacation and want to back up your photos. Open the Google Photos app and select the images you wish to upload. You can also set Google Drive to automatically sync photos from your camera roll to a dedicated folder.

Scenario 2: Uploading Scanned Documents

If you need to upload a signed document or a receipt, use your phone's camera or a scanning app like Google Drive's built-in scanner. Tap the "+" button, choose "Scan," and capture the document. Adjust the crop and save it as a PDF or image file.

Scenario 3: Uploading Audio Files

For musicians or journalists, uploading audio files directly from a recording app to Google Drive can be essential. Navigate to the file in your recording app and share it to Drive via the "Upload" option.

Troubleshooting Mobile Upload Issues

While Google Drive's mobile app is robust, you may encounter occasional hiccups during the upload process. Here's how to address them:

- **Slow Upload Speeds:** Ensure you're connected to a strong Wi-Fi network. Clear unnecessary apps running in the background to improve device performance.

- **File Format Not Supported:** Check Google Drive's supported file formats. If necessary, convert the file using a third-party app before uploading.

- **Insufficient Storage Space:** Review your Drive storage quota and delete or upgrade as needed.

- **Failed Uploads:** Restart the app or your device. If the issue persists, uninstall and reinstall the Google Drive app.

Advanced Features for On-the-Go Uploads

1. Automatic Camera Uploads

Enable Google Photos or a third-party app to sync your photos and videos directly to a designated Google Drive folder. This ensures your media is always backed up without manual intervention.

2. Integration with Other Apps

Many mobile apps offer direct integration with Google Drive, allowing you to upload files without leaving the app. For example, you can save attachments from Gmail or export files from document editors directly to your Drive.

3. File Sharing After Upload

Once your file is uploaded, share it immediately with others. Tap the file, select the "Share" option, and adjust permissions to allow others to view, comment, or edit.

Conclusion

Uploading files on the go is one of the most convenient and powerful features of Google Drive's mobile app. With a few taps, you can ensure your files are safely stored in the cloud, ready for access anytime, anywhere. By mastering these techniques, you'll enhance your productivity and make the most of your mobile device.

Ready to take it further? Explore the next section to learn how to automate tasks using Google Drive add-ons!

7.3 Automating Tasks with Google Drive Add-ons

Google Drive is not just a storage platform; it's also a robust workspace that supports automation through various add-ons. These tools extend the functionality of Google Drive, enabling users to streamline tasks, improve productivity, and reduce repetitive manual work. This section explores how you can use add-ons effectively to automate and simplify your workflow.

What Are Google Drive Add-ons?

Google Drive add-ons are third-party applications or scripts that integrate directly with Google Drive to add specialized features or automation capabilities. These tools are designed to complement Google Drive's native functionality and can be accessed via the Google Workspace Marketplace.

For instance, you can use add-ons to:

- Automatically organize files into specific folders.

- Send scheduled emails with attachments from Drive.

- Convert files into different formats automatically.

- Generate reports based on data stored in Google Sheets.

The possibilities are endless, making add-ons a valuable resource for anyone looking to boost efficiency.

Finding and Installing Add-ons

1. **Accessing the Google Workspace Marketplace**

   o   Open Google Drive and click on the gear icon in the top-right corner.

   o   Select **Get add-ons** to navigate to the Google Workspace Marketplace.

2. **Browsing Add-ons**

- o Use the search bar to find specific add-ons based on keywords like "automation" or "file management."

- o Browse through categories such as productivity, education, or business tools to discover new capabilities.

3. **Installing Add-ons**

- o Click on the desired add-on to view its details.

- o Select **Install**, grant the required permissions, and follow the on-screen instructions.

4. **Managing Installed Add-ons**

- o Access and manage your installed add-ons by navigating to the **Manage Add-ons** section in the same menu.

Popular Add-ons for Automation

Here are some widely used Google Drive add-ons to consider for automating tasks:

1. **DocuSign**

- o Automates document signing by integrating e-signature functionality directly into Google Drive.

- o Ideal for workflows involving contracts, approvals, and other signature-required tasks.

2. **AutoCrat**

- o Merges data from Google Sheets into documents or PDFs, automating the creation of invoices, certificates, and reports.

- o Offers options to email completed files automatically.

3. **Form Publisher**

- o Converts Google Forms responses into structured documents such as invoices, proposals, or certificates.

4. **Yet Another Mail Merge (YAMM)**

   o Automates email campaigns by sending personalized emails directly from Google Sheets.

5. **Kabot**

   o Simplifies file organization by automating folder creation and file sorting based on pre-defined rules.

Use Cases for Automating Tasks

1. Automating File Organization

- Use add-ons like Kabot or Google Apps Script to create rules for file naming and folder placement.

- Example: Automatically move all invoices with a specific keyword into a designated folder.

2. Automating Report Generation

- Leverage AutoCrat to pull data from spreadsheets and generate PDFs or Word documents.

- Example: Monthly sales reports can be auto-generated and emailed to stakeholders.

3. Automating Email Communication

- With YAMM, you can send out batch emails, such as event invitations, while pulling recipient details from a Google Sheet.

4. Automating Data Backups

- Use add-ons like Backupify to automate the backup of important files from Google Drive to other cloud storage services.

5. Scheduling Repeated Tasks

- Add-ons like Google Calendar Integration can set reminders or schedules based on files stored in Google Drive.

Custom Automation with Google Apps Script

For users seeking greater customization, Google Apps Script offers a powerful scripting platform to automate tasks beyond the capabilities of pre-built add-ons.

1. **What is Google Apps Script?**

   o A cloud-based JavaScript platform for customizing Google Workspace apps, including Google Drive.

2. **Getting Started**

   o Open a script editor: Navigate to **Extensions > Apps Script** in a Google Sheet, Doc, or other Drive file.

   o Write a script to automate tasks such as file renaming, scheduled sharing, or data analysis.

3. **Example Script: Organizing Files by Date**

4. function organizeFilesByDate() {

5. var folder = DriveApp.getFolderById("your-folder-id");

6. var files = folder.getFiles();

7. while (files.hasNext()) {

8. var file = files.next();

9. var date = file.getDateCreated();

10. var dateFolderName = Utilities.formatDate(date, Session.getScriptTimeZone(), "yyyy-MM-dd");

11. var dateFolder = folder.createFolder(dateFolderName);

12. file.moveTo(dateFolder);

13. }

14. }

15. **Deploying Scripts**

   o   Once the script is written, deploy it as a standalone app or trigger it to run
       at regular intervals using time-based triggers.

Tips for Successful Automation

- **Start Small**: Focus on automating a single repetitive task before tackling complex
  workflows.

- **Test Thoroughly**: Before relying on an add-on or script, test it in a controlled
  environment to ensure it works as expected.

- **Regularly Update Add-ons**: Ensure your add-ons are updated to the latest
  version to avoid compatibility issues.

- **Monitor Permissions**: Only install add-ons from trusted developers and review
  the permissions they require.

Limitations of Google Drive Add-ons

While add-ons are powerful, they come with some limitations:

- **Permission Restrictions**: Some add-ons require extensive permissions, which
  might be a concern for sensitive data.

- **Storage and Performance**: Automation may slow down if your Drive is nearing
  storage capacity.

- **Dependency on Internet Connectivity**: Many add-ons require a stable internet
  connection to function properly.

By integrating Google Drive add-ons and leveraging their automation capabilities, you can significantly boost productivity and streamline your workflows. Whether you're organizing files, generating reports, or simplifying communication, these tools are invaluable for maximizing your efficiency with Google Drive.

CHAPTER VIII
Troubleshooting and FAQs

8.1 Common Issues and Fixes

Google Drive is an intuitive and user-friendly tool, but like any software, users may occasionally encounter issues. This section provides solutions to some of the most common problems faced by Google Drive users. Whether you are dealing with sync errors, access issues, or file upload problems, these troubleshooting steps will help you resolve them quickly.

Sync Issues

One of the most common problems with Google Drive involves syncing files between devices or the cloud. Here are some potential causes and solutions:

Problem 1: Files Are Not Syncing Across Devices

- **Cause**: Internet connectivity issues or sync settings may be disabled.

- **Solution**:

    1. Ensure you are connected to a stable internet connection.

    2. Verify that syncing is enabled by checking the Google Drive desktop application.

    3. Restart the Google Drive app or refresh your browser if using the web version.

    4. Check if the file is located in the correct folder designated for syncing.

Problem 2: Google Drive Sync Is Stuck or Paused

- **Cause**: Background processes or insufficient system resources may interfere.

- **Solution**:

1. Restart your device to clear any stuck processes.

2. Ensure there is enough storage space on your local device.

3. Update your Google Drive app to the latest version to avoid bugs.

4. Check if there are any ongoing issues with Google Drive by visiting the Google Workspace Status Dashboard.

Problem 3: Duplicate Files Are Appearing After Syncing

- **Cause**: Sync conflicts due to multiple edits on the same file.

- **Solution**:

  1. Use the "Version History" feature in Google Drive to identify the latest changes.

  2. Manually review and consolidate the duplicate files if necessary.

File Upload Issues

Uploading files is one of the most essential functions of Google Drive, and encountering issues here can be frustrating.

Problem 1: Files Won't Upload

- **Cause**: Large file sizes, unsupported formats, or a slow internet connection.

- **Solution**:

  1. Check the file size limit for uploads (up to 750 GB for individual files).

  2. Compress larger files into ZIP formats to streamline uploads.

  3. Ensure the file type is supported by Google Drive.

  4. Clear your browser cache or try uploading using an incognito window.

Problem 2: Upload Is Stuck at 0% or Fails to Complete

- **Cause**: Network interruptions or browser issues.

- **Solution**:

  1. Restart your internet router or switch to a more reliable network.

2. Temporarily disable browser extensions, as they may interfere with uploads.

3. Use a different browser or upload through the Google Drive mobile app.

Problem 3: Error Message: "You Need Permission to Upload This File"

- **Cause**: The destination folder may not have appropriate permissions.

- **Solution**:

    1. Confirm that you have editing permissions for the folder where you are uploading files.

    2. Contact the folder owner to grant you the necessary access.

Access and Permissions Issues

Collaborating on Google Drive often involves sharing files and folders. Sometimes, access issues may arise.

Problem 1: Unable to Access Shared Files

- **Cause**: The file owner has not granted you the necessary permissions.

- **Solution**:

    1. Request access through the prompt provided by Google Drive.

    2. Follow up with the file owner to expedite permission approval.

    3. Verify that you are logged into the correct Google account.

Problem 2: "You Don't Have Permission to View This File" Error

- **Cause**: Changes in permissions or incorrect access links.

- **Solution**:

    1. Check the email address associated with the shared link.

    2. Request the owner to provide access or update the sharing link permissions.

    3. If you are the owner, review and adjust sharing settings under "Share."

Problem 3: File or Folder Is Missing

- **Cause**: Accidental deletion, movement, or changes in folder organization.

- **Solution**:

    1. Use the search bar in Google Drive to locate the missing item.

    2. Check the "Trash" folder for deleted files and restore them if necessary.

    3. Contact collaborators to confirm if the file was moved to a different folder.

Storage Space Issues

Limited storage can disrupt your ability to upload or sync files.

Problem 1: "Storage Full" Notification

- **Cause**: Exceeding the storage limit allocated to your Google account.

- **Solution**:

    1. Review your storage usage under "Manage Storage" in Google Drive.

    2. Delete large files, duplicates, or items in the "Trash" folder to free up space.

    3. Consider upgrading your Google One plan for additional storage.

Problem 2: Unable to Send or Receive Files via Gmail

- **Cause**: Google Drive storage is linked to Gmail and Google Photos.

- **Solution**:

    1. Clear old email attachments and photos that are taking up space.

    2. Compress or archive files to reduce storage usage.

File Format and Compatibility Issues

While Google Drive supports a wide range of file formats, there may be occasional compatibility problems.

Problem 1: Unable to Open Certain Files

- **Cause**: Unsupported file formats or missing applications.

- **Solution**:

1. Convert unsupported files into a compatible format using online tools.

2. Install necessary software or apps for proprietary formats like CAD or Photoshop.

Problem 2: Formatting Issues When Opening Microsoft Office Files

- **Cause**: Differences in formatting between Google Workspace and Microsoft Office.

- **Solution**:

    1. Use the "Office Editing" feature in Google Drive to maintain formatting.

    2. Save files in PDF format for universal compatibility.

General Performance Issues

Occasionally, Google Drive may be slow or unresponsive.

Problem 1: Slow Loading Times

- **Cause**: Browser cache or excessive open tabs.

- **Solution**:

    1. Clear your browser's cache and cookies.

    2. Close unused tabs or applications that may be consuming resources.

    3. Switch to a lighter browser like Chrome or Firefox.

Problem 2: Google Drive Freezes or Crashes

- **Cause**: Outdated software or conflicting apps.

- **Solution**:

    1. Update your browser and Google Drive application to the latest version.

    2. Temporarily disable antivirus software to test for conflicts.

Conclusion

Most Google Drive issues can be resolved with basic troubleshooting steps. Understanding the root cause of a problem and using the appropriate fixes will help you get back to being productive in no time. For persistent or uncommon issues, refer to the next section (*8.3 Where to Get Help*) for additional support resources.

8.2 Managing Storage Space

Google Drive offers a generous amount of free storage, but as you use the platform to store more files, it's possible to run out of space. Managing your storage effectively ensures you can continue using Google Drive without interruptions. This section covers strategies and tools for monitoring and optimizing your Google Drive storage usage.

8.2.1 Viewing Your Storage Usage

Knowing how much storage you have used and where it is allocated is the first step in managing your Google Drive effectively. Fortunately, Google provides built-in tools that give you a clear overview of your storage usage.

Understanding Google Drive Storage Limits

By default, Google Drive provides users with **15GB of free storage**. This space is shared across Google Drive, Gmail, and Google Photos. If you're using a Google Workspace or enterprise account, your storage limit may be higher, depending on the plan.

- **What Counts Towards Your Storage?**
    1. **Google Drive Files:** Files uploaded to Drive, including PDFs, videos, and images, count toward your storage.
    2. **Gmail Attachments:** Emails and their attachments in Gmail consume space.
    3. **Google Photos:** High-resolution photos and videos stored in Google Photos can also use your storage quota.

- **What Doesn't Count?**
    1. Google Docs, Sheets, Slides, Forms, and Jamboard files created within Google Drive do not count against your quota.

2. Files in "Shared with Me" are stored under the owner's account, not yours, unless you copy them to your Drive.

How to View Your Storage Usage

To effectively manage your storage, it's essential to regularly check how much you've used and what is consuming the most space. Here's how to do it:

1. **Using the Web Interface**

    o Open your Google Drive on a web browser.

    o At the bottom left corner of the screen, you'll see your storage bar. This displays the percentage of storage used. Click on it to get more details.

    o Alternatively, visit the **Google One storage management page** (one.google.com/storage) for a breakdown of your usage.

2. **Viewing via the Mobile App**

    o Open the Google Drive app.

    o Tap the menu (three horizontal lines) at the top left.

    o Under "Storage," you'll see how much space you've used and the total available.

3. **Using Google One App**

    o Download and install the Google One app on your mobile device.

    o Open the app to view your current storage usage across all Google services, including Gmail and Google Photos.

Breaking Down Your Storage Usage

Once you access the storage details, you'll find a categorized breakdown of where your space is being consumed. Here's what you can expect:

- **Large Files:** Google Drive highlights files that occupy significant space, making it easy to identify and delete them.

- **Trash Bin:** Files in the Trash folder still count towards your storage until permanently deleted.

- **Gmail Attachments:** Sorting emails with large attachments can free up a surprising amount of space.

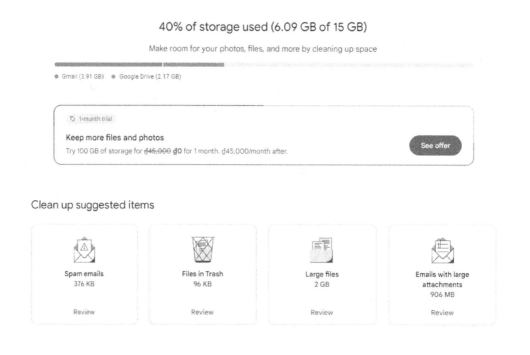

Best Practices for Monitoring Storage

1. **Enable Notifications for Storage Limits:**

    Google sends notifications when you approach your storage cap. Pay attention to these alerts to avoid interruptions in uploading or saving files.

2. **Regularly Audit Your Drive:**
    Periodically review your storage usage to ensure it aligns with your needs.

3. **Sort Files by Size:**

   In Google Drive, use the "Storage" section to sort files by size. This helps identify the largest files taking up space.

4. **Use Third-Party Tools for Insights:**

   Some tools and extensions can provide additional insights into your storage usage. Examples include **Clean Drive** or **Unclouded**.

Tips for Avoiding Storage Surprises

1. **Regular Backups:** Store essential files on an external hard drive or a secondary cloud service to free up space in Google Drive.

2. **Check Gmail and Photos Regularly:** Managing your emails and photos alongside your Drive files ensures a balanced usage across services.

3. **Be Mindful of Auto-Uploads:** If you've enabled auto-backups for photos or videos, ensure you review them periodically.

This guide has equipped you with the knowledge to monitor and manage your storage usage in Google Drive. In the next section, we'll explore strategies for freeing up space when your storage is nearing its limit.

8.2.2 Freeing Up Space

Google Drive offers a generous amount of storage for its users, but it's easy to hit the limit, especially if you manage large files or use shared folders extensively. Freeing up space doesn't have to be a daunting task. With a strategic approach and the right tools, you can efficiently reclaim space and keep your Drive organized. This section provides step-by-step guidance and tips to help you optimize your storage.

Understand What's Taking Up Space

Before you start deleting files, it's essential to know which ones are consuming the most storage. Google Drive allows you to quickly identify these files:

1. **Use the Storage Breakdown**

   o Navigate to the **Storage** section in your Drive (accessible via the left-hand menu or drive.google.com/settings/storage).

   o Here, you'll see a list of files sorted by size, making it easy to locate and prioritize large files.

2. **Inspect Shared Files**

   o Files shared with you may not count against your storage, but if you've made copies of them, those duplicates will. Check the **Shared with Me** section for redundant copies.

Delete Unnecessary Files

Deleting files is the simplest way to free up space. However, a targeted approach ensures you're not removing critical files:

1. **Old or Irrelevant Files**

   o Review files that are no longer useful, such as old presentations, outdated documents, or completed projects.

2. **Temporary Files**

   o Some files, like drafts or backups, are only necessary for a short time. Remove these if they're no longer needed.

3. **Duplicates**

   o Use Google Drive's search bar to find duplicates by searching for similar file names or extensions. Alternatively, third-party tools like **Duplicate Cleaner for Drive** can automate this process.

4. **Trash Cleanup**

- Deleting a file doesn't immediately free up space; it moves the file to the Trash. To permanently delete items:

  - Open the **Trash** folder in Drive.

  - Click **Empty Trash** or individually delete files you no longer need.

Convert Files to Save Space

Certain file types can take up significant storage. Google Drive offers conversion options to optimize your files:

1. **Convert Uploaded Files to Google Formats**

   - Non-Google file types (e.g., Microsoft Word, Excel, PDF) consume more storage. Convert them to Google Docs, Sheets, or Slides by opening the file and selecting **File > Save as Google Docs/Sheets/Slides**. These formats don't count against your storage quota.

2. **Compress Images and Videos**

   - Large media files can be resized or compressed before uploading. Tools like **TinyPNG** or video compression software can significantly reduce file sizes without noticeable quality loss.

Manage Email and Attachments

If you use Gmail, attachments saved to your Drive also consume storage. Follow these tips to manage them:

1. **Clear Large Attachments**

   - In Gmail, search for emails with large attachments by using the query: has:attachment larger:10M. Review these emails and delete unnecessary ones.

2. **Unlink Automatic Save Settings**

    o   Gmail may automatically save attachments to your Drive. To disable this, go to **Settings > General > Attachments** in Gmail and adjust the settings.

Optimize Google Photos Storage

If your Google Photos account is linked to Drive, it may consume a significant portion of your storage:

1. **Switch to "Storage Saver" Mode**

   o   This mode compresses photos and videos to reduce their size without major quality loss. Access this option through photos.google.com/settings.

2. **Delete Duplicates and Screenshots**

   o   Regularly review your photo library to remove unnecessary screenshots, blurry photos, or duplicates.

Archive or Backup Files

For files you don't need immediate access to but want to keep, consider alternative storage options:

1. **Download and Archive Locally**

   o   Transfer infrequently used files to an external hard drive or local storage.

2. **Use Other Cloud Services**

   o   Services like Dropbox or OneDrive can supplement your Google Drive storage.

3. **Google Takeout**

   o   Use Google Takeout to download a complete archive of your Drive data for safekeeping before deleting older files.

Upgrade Your Storage Plan

If you've exhausted all space-saving measures and still need more room, upgrading your Google Drive storage might be the best option. Google offers flexible plans:

- **Google One Plans**: Start with 100 GB and go up to 2 TB or more, depending on your needs.

- **Family Sharing**: Share storage with family members to maximize value.

Automation for Long-Term Space Management

Finally, maintaining your storage space over time requires consistency. Here are some automation tips:

1. **Set Reminders for Cleanup**

   o   Use Google Calendar to schedule monthly reminders to review your Drive.

2. **Use Third-Party Cleanup Tools**

   o   Apps like **Clean Drive** or **Drive Organizer** can help automate the identification and removal of unnecessary files.

3. **Enable Automatic Deletion for Trash**

   o   Files in the Trash are automatically deleted after 30 days, ensuring you don't need to clean it manually.

Conclusion

Freeing up space in Google Drive is an ongoing process that requires regular attention. By combining proactive file management, smart conversion techniques, and strategic archiving, you can keep your Drive clutter-free and efficient. The steps outlined above not only help you regain storage but also foster better organization, making it easier to locate and manage your files. Whether you're a casual user or a power user, these tips will ensure your Google Drive remains an indispensable tool in your digital toolkit.

8.3 Where to Get Help

When using Google Drive, it's natural to encounter questions or issues that require assistance. Whether you're troubleshooting a technical glitch, learning a new feature, or seeking best practices, there are plenty of resources available to help you navigate and master Google Drive. In this section, we'll explore the most effective ways to get help, including Google's official support channels, community forums, and other external resources.

Google Support Center

The **Google Support Center** is the first and most comprehensive place to look for help. Google has curated a vast library of articles, tutorials, and step-by-step guides covering every feature of Google Drive. Here's how to make the most of it:

- **Navigating the Support Center**: Visit the Google Drive Help page (https://support.google.com/drive) and use the search bar to look up specific issues. Common topics include file recovery, sharing permissions, and syncing issues.

- **Step-by-Step Guides**: Many articles feature detailed instructions accompanied by screenshots, making it easy to follow along.

- **Troubleshooting Tools**: Some articles link to automated tools or diagnostic pages that can help identify and fix problems, such as storage management or file access errors.

Pro Tip: Bookmark the Google Drive Help page for quick access whenever you need assistance.

In-App Help and Feedback Tools

Google Drive also integrates help and feedback options directly within its interface. These tools are designed to provide instant guidance without leaving the app.

- **Help Menu**:
    o Click on the question mark (?) icon located in the upper-right corner of the Google Drive interface.
    o Use the search bar to look up your query, or browse suggested help topics.
    o The results often include direct links to relevant support articles.

- **Send Feedback**:
    o If you encounter a bug or have suggestions for improvement, click on the "Help & Feedback" option.
    o Provide detailed information about your issue or suggestion. Google often reviews this feedback to improve their services.

Google Community Forums

The **Google Drive Community Forum** is a vibrant space where users and experts gather to share tips, answer questions, and discuss common issues.

- **How to Access**: Navigate to https://support.google.com/drive/community to explore threads or post your own question.

- **Benefits of Forums**:
    - Receive advice from experienced users and Google product experts.
    - Discover solutions to uncommon problems not covered in official documentation.
    - Engage in discussions about best practices and creative ways to use Google Drive.

Pro Tip: When posting a question, include as many details as possible, such as the device you're using, the browser version, and a clear description of the issue.

YouTube Tutorials and Online Guides

For visual learners, YouTube is an excellent resource for Google Drive help. Many tech educators and enthusiasts create video tutorials to explain features and solve problems.

- **Google's Official YouTube Channel**: Google Workspace's YouTube channel often publishes videos highlighting new features or providing quick tips.

- **Independent Creators**: Search YouTube for specific tutorials, such as "How to Recover Deleted Files in Google Drive" or "How to Use Google Drive Offline."

- **Benefits of Video Tutorials**: Watching a step-by-step process can make it easier to understand complex tasks.

Social Media Support

Google actively engages with users on social media platforms, offering another way to seek assistance.

- **Twitter**: Follow and reach out to @Google or @GoogleWorkspace. You can ask quick questions or check for updates on ongoing issues.

- **LinkedIn**: Google Drive experts often share tips and updates on LinkedIn. Joining Google Workspace-related groups can also provide insights and advice.

External Blogs and Third-Party Resources

While Google's official support is highly reliable, many third-party blogs and websites offer valuable tips and tricks for using Google Drive more effectively.

- **Tech Blogs**: Websites like TechRadar, CNET, and How-To Geek frequently publish articles about Google Drive updates and tutorials.

- **User Communities**: Join forums such as Reddit's r/google or r/techsupport to ask questions and explore solutions shared by tech-savvy individuals.

Professional IT Support

For businesses or organizations using Google Workspace, professional IT support may be the best option for resolving complex issues.

- **Google Workspace Admin Help**: If you're part of an organization, contact your IT administrator for support. They have access to advanced troubleshooting tools and direct communication channels with Google support teams.

- **Third-Party IT Providers**: Many managed IT service providers specialize in Google Workspace solutions and can assist with integration, security, and technical issues.

Paid Support Options

If you require premium support, Google offers paid options for its Workspace customers.

- **Priority Support**: Available for Google Workspace Business and Enterprise plans, priority support provides faster response times and access to advanced troubleshooting.

- **Support Tiers**: Review your Workspace plan to understand the level of support included, and consider upgrading if your business requires enhanced assistance.

When to Contact Google Support Directly

While many issues can be resolved through self-help resources, some problems require direct assistance from Google.

- **Contact Options**:
    - Use the "Contact Us" button on the Google Drive Help page.
    - Choose from options such as email support, live chat, or phone assistance (depending on your location and plan).

- **When to Contact Google**:
    - Account recovery issues (e.g., forgotten passwords or hacked accounts).
    - Payment or billing inquiries for additional storage.
    - Data loss or suspected unauthorized access to your files.

Final Thoughts

No matter the issue, rest assured that help is readily available when using Google Drive. From the robust Support Center to community forums, and even direct assistance, Google provides a wealth of resources to ensure you have a seamless experience. By leveraging these tools and platforms, you can quickly overcome obstacles and continue using Google Drive with confidence.

Conclusion

Recap of Key Features

Google Drive is a versatile tool that combines cloud storage, file sharing, and productivity features in one seamless platform. In this recap, we'll revisit the key features that make Google Drive an essential tool for users of all skill levels, whether you're a student, professional, or just someone looking to organize your digital life.

1. Easy Access Anywhere, Anytime

Google Drive's cloud-based system allows you to access your files from virtually anywhere with an internet connection. Whether you're on a desktop, laptop, tablet, or smartphone, your documents, presentations, photos, and spreadsheets are always at your fingertips. This accessibility ensures you can work remotely, collaborate with team members worldwide, or simply retrieve a document on the go.

Key Highlights:

- **Cross-Device Compatibility:** Your files are synchronized across all devices using the same Google account.

- **Offline Access:** With a bit of setup, you can work on your files offline, and changes will sync automatically when you're back online.

- **Mobile App:** The Google Drive app for iOS and Android provides a streamlined experience for managing files on the go.

2. Intuitive File Organization

Google Drive makes it simple to organize your files with its folder-based system. You can create folders to categorize your files, move them around with drag-and-drop functionality, and even color-code folders for easy visual identification.

Key Highlights:

- **Customizable Folders:** Organize by project, client, subject, or any system that works for you.

- **Search Functionality:** Google's powerful search engine is integrated into Drive, making it easy to find files by name, type, or even content within a document.

- **Priority Section:** Quickly access files that are most relevant or frequently used.

3. Seamless Sharing and Collaboration

Collaboration is one of Google Drive's standout features. Sharing files and folders is straightforward, allowing you to grant access to specific individuals or groups. The collaboration tools go beyond basic sharing, enabling multiple users to edit, comment on, and work on files in real-time.

Key Highlights:

- **Flexible Sharing Options:** Choose between view-only, comment-only, or full editing permissions.

- **Real-Time Collaboration:** See others' edits live, eliminating version control issues.

- **Activity Tracking:** Keep tabs on who has accessed or edited a file.

4. Integrated Productivity Tools

Google Drive is much more than a storage solution. Its integration with Google Workspace tools—such as Docs, Sheets, and Slides—turns it into a powerful productivity hub.

Key Highlights:

- **Google Docs:** Create text documents with collaborative editing, formatting options, and comments.

- **Google Sheets:** Develop spreadsheets with advanced functions, data visualization, and collaborative tools.

- **Google Slides:** Design professional presentations with templates, animations, and transitions.

- **Add-ons and Extensions:** Extend functionality with third-party apps and tools.

5. Advanced Features for Power Users

As you gain confidence in using Google Drive, its advanced features can help streamline your workflow and boost productivity.

Key Highlights:

- **Version History:** Easily view and restore previous versions of files.

- **Add-ons and Integrations:** Expand Google Drive's capabilities by integrating with third-party tools like Trello, Adobe, and Zoom.

- **Shared Drives:** Perfect for team projects, allowing centralized file access and management.

- **File Conversion:** Seamlessly convert Microsoft Office files to Google formats and vice versa.

6. Robust Security and Privacy Controls

Keeping your data secure is a priority with Google Drive. With various built-in security features, you can confidently store and share sensitive information.

Key Highlights:

- **Encryption:** All files are encrypted in transit and at rest.

- **Access Controls:** Decide who can view, edit, or comment on your files.

- **Two-Factor Authentication:** Add an extra layer of security to your account.

7. Storage Management

Google Drive offers generous storage options to fit different needs. While free accounts come with 15 GB of space shared across Google services, you can upgrade to Google One for additional storage.

Key Highlights:

- **Storage Overview:** Easily track how much space you've used and what types of files are taking up space.

- **Clean-Up Tools:** Quickly identify large or unnecessary files with Google's storage manager.

- **Flexible Plans:** Choose a storage plan that fits your needs, starting at 100 GB and scaling to several terabytes.

8. Integration with Google Ecosystem

One of the biggest strengths of Google Drive is its seamless integration with other Google services.

Key Highlights:

- **Google Calendar:** Attach files directly to events for easy access during meetings.
- **Google Keep:** Store notes and attach them to related files.
- **Google Photos:** Automatically back up and organize your photos and videos.

9. User-Friendly Interface

Google Drive's interface is designed for simplicity and ease of use. Even if you're a beginner, the clean layout and logical organization ensure a smooth learning curve.

Key Highlights:

- **Drag-and-Drop Functionality:** Easily upload or rearrange files.
- **Quick Access Panel:** See recently opened files at a glance.
- **Help and Support:** Access guides and troubleshooting tips directly from the interface.

10. Cost-Effective Solution

For personal users, the free plan provides ample storage and functionality. Businesses and professionals can benefit from premium plans with enhanced features, making Google Drive a cost-effective solution for individuals and teams alike.

Final Thoughts

These key features demonstrate why Google Drive is a reliable and versatile tool for storing, sharing, and managing digital content. As you continue to use it, you'll discover even more ways to leverage its capabilities to simplify your life and enhance your productivity.

Let Google Drive be your go-to platform for staying organized, collaborating efficiently, and accessing your files whenever and wherever you need them. Explore its features further and unlock its full potential for your personal or professional projects.

Encouragement to Explore Further

As you close the pages of this book, your journey with Google Drive is just beginning. The platform offers an expansive world of tools, features, and integrations that can help you organize, collaborate, and innovate like never before. In this section, we aim to inspire you to take your newfound knowledge and explore even further, making Google Drive an indispensable part of your personal and professional life.

Harness the Power of Experimentation

The best way to truly master Google Drive is by experimenting. Don't be afraid to try new features, even if they seem advanced or unfamiliar at first. For instance:

- **Experiment with Add-ons**: Add-ons like DocuSign for electronic signatures or Workona for advanced tab management can elevate your productivity.

- **Test Advanced Search Features**: Learn to refine your searches using operators like "type:pdf" or "owner:me" to find exactly what you need.

- **Explore Integrations**: Syncing with apps like Trello, Asana, or Slack can make your workflows smoother and more cohesive.

By experimenting, you'll uncover hidden gems that align with your unique needs and goals.

Make Google Drive Your Digital Hub

Think of Google Drive as the central hub for your digital life. Whether you're organizing personal documents, managing team projects, or brainstorming creative ideas, Drive can accommodate it all. Here are some suggestions to deepen your engagement:

- **Create Templates for Efficiency**: Use Google Docs or Sheets to design templates for recurring tasks, like monthly reports or project trackers.

- **Build Collaborative Workspaces**: Set up shared folders for teams or groups to keep everyone aligned and ensure seamless collaboration.

- **Leverage Cloud Accessibility**: Access and edit your files on any device, making Drive a reliable companion for travel or remote work.

Stay Updated on New Features

Google is continually enhancing Drive with new capabilities. To stay ahead, make it a habit to:

- **Follow Google's Official Updates**: Regularly check Google Workspace's blog or YouTube channel for announcements and tutorials.

- **Join Online Communities**: Engage with forums like Reddit or Google Drive-focused Facebook groups to share tips and tricks with other users.

- **Explore Beta Programs**: Occasionally, Google offers beta access to upcoming features—don't hesitate to sign up and get an early look.

Expand Your Knowledge Through Learning

Mastery comes from a commitment to continuous learning. Here's how you can grow your expertise with Google Drive:

- **Take Online Courses**: Platforms like Coursera, Udemy, and LinkedIn Learning often offer courses focused on Google Drive and its integrations.

- **Read Blogs and Tutorials**: Many tech enthusiasts and professionals share in-depth guides, case studies, and hacks online.

- **Watch Tutorials**: YouTube is brimming with free video tutorials that walk you through both basic and advanced features step by step.

Integrate Google Drive Into Your Long-Term Goals

Google Drive isn't just a tool; it's a means to achieve your broader aspirations. Whether you're:

- **Launching a Business**: Use Drive to draft business plans, track budgets in Sheets, and share proposals with partners.

- **Advancing Your Career**: Develop your professional brand by storing a polished resume, portfolio, and key documents in Drive.

- **Pursuing Personal Projects**: From organizing family photos to managing creative writing projects, Drive can support your passions.

Overcome Challenges with Confidence

It's natural to encounter challenges as you explore further. Maybe a file isn't syncing correctly, or you're unsure how to optimize storage space. Remember that help is always available:

- **Consult Google's Help Center**: This resource offers comprehensive guides and FAQs to resolve most issues.

- **Reach Out to Support**: For more complex concerns, Google Support provides direct assistance through chat, email, or phone.

- **Learn From Others**: Online forums and social media groups can be invaluable for troubleshooting and advice.

Inspire Others to Use Google Drive

As you grow more comfortable with Google Drive, consider sharing your knowledge. Whether it's teaching a friend how to create folders or conducting a workshop at work, helping others unlock the power of Drive can be rewarding. Plus, teaching is one of the best ways to reinforce your own learning.

Closing Thoughts

Google Drive is more than just a cloud storage solution—it's a platform that empowers you to manage, create, and collaborate with ease. By embracing its potential, you'll not only simplify your daily life but also open doors to new opportunities and achievements.

So, go ahead. Experiment with features, explore integrations, and engage with the Google Drive community. The more you invest in learning and using this tool, the more it will reward you with efficiency, creativity, and organization. Your journey with Google Drive is just beginning—let it take you further than you ever imagined.

Appendices

Appendix A: Google Drive Keyboard Shortcuts

Google Drive offers a range of keyboard shortcuts that can dramatically speed up your workflow and make navigation more efficient. Whether you're a beginner or an advanced user, knowing these shortcuts will help you work smarter, not harder. This appendix is your go-to guide for mastering the essential keyboard shortcuts in Google Drive.

1. Why Use Keyboard Shortcuts?

Keyboard shortcuts are a powerful way to save time and reduce repetitive actions. Here are some key benefits:

- **Efficiency**: Perform tasks in seconds without navigating through menus.
- **Focus**: Stay engaged in your workflow without breaking concentration.
- **Accessibility**: Improve usability, especially for users with motor impairments.

2. How to Access the Shortcut Guide in Google Drive

Google Drive has a built-in shortcut guide you can quickly reference:

1. Open Google Drive in your browser.
2. Press **Shift + ?** to display a complete list of available shortcuts.
3. Use the scroll bar or arrow keys to navigate through the guide.

3. General Navigation Shortcuts

These shortcuts help you move around Google Drive effortlessly:

Shortcut	Action
G then N	Go to the "My Drive" section.
G then S	Open the "Shared with Me" folder.
G then R	View "Recent" files.

G then A	Go to "Starred" files.
G then T	Navigate to the Trash folder.
/ (Forward Slash)	Open the search bar.

4. File and Folder Management

Speed up actions like creating, renaming, or deleting files:

Shortcut	Action
C	Create a new file.
Shift + T	Create a new Google Doc.
Shift + S	Create a new Google Sheet.
Shift + P	Create a new Google Slide.
N	Rename a selected file or folder.
Delete	Move selected files to Trash.
Shift + Z	Add a shortcut to a selected file.

5. File Viewing and Selection

Manage files in your Drive more effectively:

Shortcut	Action
Enter	Open a selected file or folder.
Shift + Enter	Preview a file.
J or K	Move up or down through files.
X	Select or deselect a file.
A	Select all items in a folder.
Shift + A	Deselect all items.

6. Collaboration and Sharing

Simplify sharing and working with others:

Shortcut	Action
. (Period)	Open the Share settings for a file.
S	Add or remove a star on a file.
Shift + F	Add a selected file to a folder.

7. Search and Filter

Find files quickly with these shortcuts:

Shortcut	Action
/ (Forward Slash)	Open the search bar.
Alt + /	Access help in the search bar.
Q	Filter files by type.

8. Accessibility Shortcuts

For users relying on screen readers or other accessibility tools:

Shortcut	Action
Ctrl + Alt + Z	Toggle screen reader support.
Ctrl + Alt + /	Open accessibility settings.

9. Offline Mode Shortcuts

If you use Google Drive offline, the following shortcuts remain functional:

Shortcut	Action
Enter	Open an offline file.
Ctrl + S	Save changes offline.

10. Mobile App Shortcuts

While mobile devices lack traditional keyboard shortcuts, the Google Drive app offers gesture-based equivalents:

- **Swipe right**: Star a file.
- **Swipe left**: Move a file to Trash.
- **Tap and hold**: Access multi-file selection.

11. Tips for Mastering Keyboard Shortcuts

1. **Start Small**: Focus on learning 3-5 shortcuts at a time.
2. **Practice Often**: Repetition will help you remember them.
3. **Create a Cheat Sheet**: Print out this appendix or jot down key shortcuts.
4. **Use Tools**: Many browser extensions and apps can help you memorize shortcuts.

12. Most Popular Shortcuts

Based on user feedback, the following shortcuts are the most frequently used:

- **Shift + ?**: Open the shortcut guide.

- **C**: Create a new file.

- **/ (Forward Slash)**: Search files.

- **N**: Rename files.

- **Delete**: Move to Trash.

Keyboard shortcuts are a gateway to using Google Drive like a pro. Commit these to memory or keep this appendix handy to transform your workflow and maximize productivity.

Appendix B: Glossary of Terms

This glossary is designed to help beginners understand common terms and concepts used in Google Drive. Each entry includes a clear definition and, where applicable, examples or explanations of how the term relates to Google Drive.

A

Add-ons: Optional tools or features that can be integrated with Google Drive to extend its functionality. Examples include Google Workspace Marketplace tools for automation or productivity.
Archive: A process or location to store files that are no longer frequently accessed but are kept for future reference.

B

Backup: A copy of your files or data stored on Google Drive to prevent loss due to hardware failure, accidental deletion, or other issues. Google Drive can be used to back up files from computers, mobile devices, and other cloud services.
Bin/Trash: A location in Google Drive where deleted files are temporarily stored. Files in the Bin can be restored within 30 days or permanently deleted sooner if needed.

C

Cloud Storage: A type of storage where files are saved on remote servers rather than local devices. Google Drive is a popular example of cloud storage, allowing users to access files from anywhere with an internet connection.
Collaboration: Working together with others on the same document, spreadsheet, or presentation in real-time. Google Drive supports collaborative features like comments, suggestions, and simultaneous editing.

D

Dashboard: The main screen in Google Drive where you can see your recent activity, uploaded files, and available storage space.
Drive File Stream: A feature that allows enterprise users to stream files directly from Google Drive to their computer without taking up local storage.

E

Encryption: A security measure that protects your files by converting them into unreadable code unless accessed with the correct credentials. Google Drive uses encryption to secure data in transit and at rest.

Explorer View: A feature in Google Drive that allows users to navigate through folders and files similar to how they would in a file manager on their computer.

F

File Sharing: The process of granting other users access to specific files or folders in Google Drive. Permissions can range from viewing only to editing or full control.

Folder: A virtual container used to organize files in Google Drive. Folders can be nested within other folders to create a hierarchical structure.

G

Google Workspace: A suite of productivity tools including Google Drive, Docs, Sheets, Slides, Gmail, and more. Formerly known as G Suite.

Granular Permissions: Detailed access settings that allow file owners to control what specific users can do with shared files (e.g., view, comment, edit).

H

History (Version History): A feature that allows users to see past versions of a document, spreadsheet, or presentation. Version history helps track changes and restore previous versions if needed.

I

Integration: The process of connecting Google Drive with other tools or platforms, such as Slack, Zoom, or Microsoft Office, to streamline workflows.

Instant Upload: The ability to automatically upload photos, videos, or files from a mobile device to Google Drive as they are created.

K

Keyboard Shortcuts: Quick key combinations that allow users to perform specific actions in Google Drive more efficiently. For example, pressing "Shift + Z" lets you add a file to multiple folders.

L

Link Sharing: A feature in Google Drive that generates a unique URL for a file or folder, which can be shared with others for quick access. Permissions can be adjusted for those using the link.

M

Metadata: Information about a file, such as its name, creation date, and last modified date. Metadata helps users organize and search for files in Google Drive.
Migration: The process of transferring files from one storage system to another, such as moving files from a local hard drive to Google Drive.

N

Notifications: Alerts or updates about changes to shared files or folders. Notifications can appear in the Google Drive interface or be sent via email.

O

Offline Mode: A feature that allows users to access and edit files in Google Drive without an internet connection. Changes are synced when the device reconnects.

P

Pinned Files: Files that are marked for quick access and displayed prominently in the Google Drive interface.
Preview: The ability to view a file without opening it in its corresponding app. Google Drive supports previews for a variety of file types, including images, PDFs, and videos.

R

Real-Time Collaboration: A feature that allows multiple users to work on the same file simultaneously, with changes visible in real time.
Restore: The process of recovering a deleted file from the Bin or reverting a document to a previous version using version history.

S

Search Bar: A tool in Google Drive that allows users to find files or folders by name, keyword, or metadata. Advanced search filters can narrow results further.
Shared Drives (formerly Team Drives): A type of Drive designed for teams to store, access, and collaborate on files collectively, with ownership tied to the organization rather than individuals.

T

Template: A pre-designed file structure available in Google Docs, Sheets, or Slides that can be customized to suit specific needs.

Third-Party Apps: External applications that can be connected to Google Drive to add additional functionality, such as PDF editing or e-signatures.

U

Upload: The process of transferring files from a local device to Google Drive for cloud storage. Files can be uploaded individually or in batches.

Usage Statistics: Data that shows how much storage space is being used and what types of files occupy the most space in Google Drive.

V

Viewer: A permission setting in Google Drive that allows users to view a file without making any changes or leaving comments.

W

Workspace: The personalized area in Google Drive where users can quickly access and organize their most-used files and folders.

Z

Zip File: A compressed file format that reduces the size of one or more files for easier storage and sharing. Google Drive can preview and unzip these files.

Acknowledgments

Thank you for choosing **Google Drive Made Simple: A Beginner's Handbook.**

I deeply appreciate your trust in this guide to help you navigate the world of Google Drive. Writing this book has been a journey fueled by the desire to simplify technology for everyone, and your decision to pick up this book means the world to me.

Whether you're a student, a professional, or someone simply looking to get more organized, I hope this book has provided you with valuable insights and tools to make Google Drive work for you. My goal was to make the learning process as straightforward and enjoyable as possible, and I sincerely hope I achieved that for you.

Your support not only helps bring books like this to life but also encourages me to continue creating resources that make technology accessible and empowering. If this book has been helpful to you, I'd love to hear your feedback. Feel free to share your thoughts or reach out with suggestions for future topics.

Once again, thank you for allowing this book to be a part of your journey toward greater productivity and digital mastery.

Wishing you success and ease in all your endeavors,

www.ingramcontent.com/pod-product-compliance
Lightning Source LLC
LaVergne TN
LVHW062314060326

832902LV00013B/2208